Marseille Travel Guide 2023: A Comprehensive Guide to the Best Things to Do, Historical Sites, Savory Food and Wine, and Off-the-Beaten-Path Adventures in the Heart of the Mediterranean

Marco Rossi

All rights reserved. No part of this publication may be reproduced, distributed, or transmitted in any form or by any means, including photocopying, recording, or other electronic or mechanical methods, without the prior written permission of the publisher, except in the case of brief quotations embodied in critical reviews and certain other noncommercial uses permitted by copyright law.

Copyright © (Marco Rossi), (2023).

Thank you for your interest in this book. Happy reading and enjoy the journey!

Table of Contents

Chapter 1: Introduction to Marseille 9
    Overview of Marseille 14
    Why Visit Marseille? 19
    Best Time to Visit 24
    How to Get to Marseille 28
    Public Transportation in Marseille 32
    Hotel and accommodations in Marseille 36
    Hotels in Marseille 40

Chapter 2: Marseille for First-Timers 45
    Top Attractions for First-Time Visitors 45
    Where to Stay in Marseille: A Neighborhood Guide .. 91
    Essential French Phrases for Travelers 95
    Safety Tips and Precautions 99

    Chapter 3: Marseille Travel Itinerary 102

    Unveiling Marseille: A 3-Day Voyage through Mediterranean Magic 102

    Marseille and Beyond: A 7-Day Odyssey Through Southern Splendor 107

    Marseille Family Adventure: A 7-Day Journey of Discovery and Fun 113

    Marseille through the Lens: A 7-Day Photography Expedition 119

Chapter 4: Hidden Gems in Marseille 124

Off-the-Beaten-Path Places to Explore 124

Lesser-Known Museums and Art Galleries 157

Secret Gardens and Parks 190

Unique Local Experiences..216

Chapter 5: Marseille's Neighborhoods 246

Le Panier: Marseille's Historic Quarter 246

La Plaine: Bohemian Vibe and Street Markets 251

Cours Julien: Artsy and Lively District 256

The Old Port (Vieux Port): The Heart of the City 260

La Corniche: Stunning Sea Views 264

Chapter 6: Must-Visit Landmarks and Attractions 267

Basilique Notre-Dame de la Garde 267

Château d'If and Frioul Archipelago....................... 271

Marseille Cathedral (Cathédrale de la Major) 275

Palais Longchamp 279

Fort Saint-Jean 283

Chapter 7: Museums and Cultural Sites 287

MuCEM (Museum of European and Mediterranean Civilizations)... 287

Musée d'Histoire de Marseille (History Museum) 291

Musée des Beaux-Arts (Fine Arts Museum)............. 295

Regards de Provence Museum 299

La Vieille Charité 303

Chapter 8: Outdoor Activities and Nature 307
  Calanques National Park: Hiking and Scenic Beauty
  307
  Frioul Archipelago: Beaches and Nature Retreat 311
  Parc Borély: Gardens and Recreational Park 315
  Watersports and Boat Tours 318
Chapter 9: Food and Dining in Marseille 322
  Introduction to Provençal Cuisine 322
  Must-Try Marseille Specialties 327
  Top Restaurants and Street Food 332
  Best Cafés and Bakeries 337
Chapter 10: Shopping in Marseille 343
  Local Markets and Flea Markets 343
  Unique Souvenirs to Bring Home 348
  High-End Shopping Districts 352
Chapter 11: Nightlife and Entertainment 356
  Bars and Pubs with a View 356
  Live Music and Concert Venues 360
  Marseille's Vibrant Nightclubs 364
Chapter 12: Practical Information 368
  Currency and Payment Methods 368
  Transportation Tips and Passes 372
  Tourist Information Centers 377

Chapter 13: Day Trips from Marseille 381

    Aix-en-Provence 381

    Cassis 387

    Avignon 393

    Arles 398

Chapter 14: Conclusion 403

    Final Tips and Recommendations 403

    Fond Farewell to Marseille 407

Chapter 1: Introduction to Marseille

The first time I set foot in Marseille, it felt like a reunion with an old friend I never knew I had. The Mediterranean breeze carried the faint scent of salt and adventure, and as I gazed out at the bustling Vieux Port, I knew I was about to embark on a journey filled with unforgettable moments.

Marseille, a city with a history that dates back to ancient Greece, welcomed me with open arms. The warm Mediterranean sun kissed my skin as I strolled along the quays, where fishermen hawked their fresh catches and jovial locals shared stories over glasses of pastis.

One evening, I found myself perched atop the iconic Basilique Notre-Dame de la Garde. The view from this hillside sanctuary was nothing short of breathtaking. As the sun dipped below the horizon, the city below transformed into a sea of twinkling lights, and the vastness of the Mediterranean stretched out before me, hinting at the adventures that awaited.

In the days that followed, I explored hidden calanques, swam in crystal-clear waters, and reveled in the intoxicating aroma of lavender and rosemary wafting through the markets. I uncovered the city's rich history, from the Roman ruins of Arles to the artistic inspirations of Vincent van Gogh in nearby Saint-Rémy-de-Provence.

But what truly stole my heart were the moments that unfolded away from the tourist trail. I was savoring bouillabaisse in a family-run restaurant tucked away in Le Panier. It was joining locals for a game of pétanque on a dusty square in Cours Julien. It was sharing stories with fishermen at the Vallon des Auffes, a hidden gem that felt like a well-kept secret.

Marseille, with its vibrant culture, ancient treasures, and Mediterranean beauty, became more than a destination—it became a part of me. It's a place where history whispers through cobblestone streets, where the sea sings its siren song, and where adventure beckons at every corner.

In this Marseille Travel Guide, I invite you to join me on a journey through this enchanting city to uncover its hidden treasures, indulge in its culinary delights, and embrace the warmth of its people. Marseille is not just a place to visit; it's a place to experience, to savor, and to fall in love with.

So, my fellow traveler, as you turn these pages and prepare for your own Marseille adventure, may this guide be your trusted companion on this remarkable journey. Marseille is waiting to unveil its magic to you, and I promise you'll leave a part of your heart in this Mediterranean gem.

Welcome to Marseille—a love story in the making.

Overview of Marseille

Marseille is a city that captures the heart and ignites the senses! As you embark on your journey through the sun-kissed Mediterranean shores, allow me to paint a vivid overview of this enchanting French gem, drawing you closer to its pulsating soul.

Picture yourself strolling along the historic Vieux Port, where boats gently sway in harmony with the sea's rhythm and the aroma of freshly caught seafood fills the air. The colorful facades of Le Panier, the oldest district, beckon you to wander through its maze-like alleys, inviting you to discover hidden treasures and charming artisan boutiques.

As you amble along the sun-dappled streets, the unmistakable scent of Provencal herbs and olive oil from nearby markets awakens your taste buds. Marseille's culinary prowess is legendary, boasting a delectable medley of bouillabaisse, a rich seafood stew that tantalizes your palate, and pastis, the anise-flavored aperitif that locals swear by.

Stepping into the heart of the city, you're greeted by the iconic Basilique Notre-Dame de la Garde, a majestic hilltop basilica that stands guard over Marseille like a watchful guardian. Its glistening gold statue of the Virgin Mary embraces the city, offering blessings and protection to those who visit.

Delving deeper into Marseille's soul, the fascinating blend of cultures becomes apparent.

Mediterranean influences intertwine with a lively North African spirit, infusing the city with a diverse and vibrant atmosphere. Arabic signs decorate storefronts, French and Occitan conversations mix in the air, and the soul-stirring sounds of traditional music echo through the streets.

As the sun sets over the horizon, the Old Port transforms into a kaleidoscope of colors. Street performers mesmerize the crowd, while artists showcase their talents on the vibrant Cours Julien square. Lively laughter and the clinking of glasses resonate from cozy cafés as the city comes alive with a sense of conviviality that's uniquely Marseille.

Beyond the urban allure lies a haven for nature enthusiasts. The Calanques, a breathtaking national park, offers a scenic sanctuary where rugged limestone cliffs meet the azure Mediterranean waters. Hiking through this majestic landscape rewards you with awe-inspiring vistas that instill a sense of wonder and humility.

Whether you seek adventure, art, or tranquility, Marseille effortlessly provides a diverse tapestry of experiences. From the cultural wonders of the MuCEM to the serene beauty of Parc Borély, each moment spent here is a captivating revelation.

With every step, Marseille unveils a part of itself, intimately inviting you to embrace its joie de vivre, its passionate spirit, and its time-honored traditions. This city casts a spell that transcends the pages of a travel guide; it becomes a cherished memory that lingers in your heart long after you bid farewell.

Marseille awaits with open arms—a cherished voyage of discovery, an embrace of authenticity, and a celebration of life's simple pleasures. So, come, let Marseille enfold you in its warm embrace, and embark on an unforgettable journey that will forever be etched in your soul.

Why Visit Marseille?

Ah, why visit Marseille? A question that is swiftly answered with an enchanting array of reasons, each more compelling than the last. Let me weave a tapestry of allure that will beckon you to this captivating city on the Mediterranean shores.

First and foremost, Marseille exudes a timeless charm born from a rich history that spans over 2,600 years. As France's oldest city, its streets whisper tales of ancient civilizations, medieval knights, and maritime glory. From the picturesque Vieux Port, where seafarers have docked for centuries, to the grandeur of the Basilique Notre-Dame de la Garde, perched atop a hill, Marseille's historical landmarks stand as testaments to its enduring legacy.

Beyond its history, Marseille embraces a vivacious multicultural spirit. It is a melting pot of cultures where French, Mediterranean, and North African influences intermingle harmoniously. The city's dynamic blend of traditions infuses every aspect of life, from its vibrant markets filled with tantalizing spices and flavors to the captivating blend of languages spoken on its streets.

For the epicurean at heart, Marseille is a true culinary delight. Prepare to savor the world-famous bouillabaisse, a gastronomic masterpiece that epitomizes the essence of the Mediterranean. Pair it with a refreshing glass of pastis and allow your taste buds to dance in delight, for Marseille's cuisine is nothing short of an exquisite love affair with food.

Nature enthusiasts will find sanctuary in the Calanques National Park, a natural wonder that lies just a stone's throw from the bustling city center. These majestic limestone cliffs, interspersed with turquoise coves, offer a playground for hikers, rock climbers, and sea lovers alike. The breathtaking vistas are nothing short of a poetic rendezvous between land and sea.

Art and culture aficionados will discover a treasure trove of museums, galleries, and street art that add a vibrant brushstroke to Marseille's canvas. From the contemporary masterpieces at MuCEM to the bohemian charm of Cours Julien, the city is a canvas for artistic expression and creative exploration.

Marseille's warm and welcoming locals, known as "Marseillais," add an intangible charm that embraces visitors like long-lost friends. Their love for their city is contagious, and their zest for life is a celebration that permeates every corner. Engage in lively conversations and immerse yourself in their festivities, and you'll leave with not just memories but cherished friendships.

Lastly, Marseille is a city that wears its heart on its sleeve. Its authenticity is raw and unfiltered, inviting travelers to experience it in all its glory—the beautiful and the imperfect, the ancient and the modern, the quiet moments and the vibrant celebrations. Marseille welcomes you with open arms, ready to offer an adventure that will leave an indelible mark on your soul.

So, dear traveler, come to Marseille, and you'll find not just a destination but a revelation—a city that encapsulates the essence of life's rich tapestry, where history, culture, and nature intertwine to create an unforgettable symphony of experiences. It's a love affair waiting to be embraced, an intoxicating journey that will etch Marseille into your heart, forever calling you back to its loving embrace.

Best Time to Visit

Choosing the best time to visit Marseille depends on your preferences for weather, events, and crowd levels. Each season brings its own unique charm to the city.

Spring (March to May)

Spring is a delightful time to visit Marseille, as the city awakens from its winter slumber. Temperatures start to warm up, and the blooming flowers add a colorful touch to the streets and parks. The city is less crowded than in the summer, making it an ideal time for sightseeing and exploring attractions without long lines. The Mistral wind, common in spring, can bring occasional gusts, so packing a light jacket is advisable. Plus, in May, you can catch the bustling Fête de la Mer (Sea Festival), celebrating the city's maritime heritage.

Summer (June to August)

If you crave a sun-soaked Mediterranean experience, summer is the season for you. Marseille is abuzz with energy as locals and tourists alike flock to the beaches and outdoor terraces. The weather is warm and inviting, perfect for swimming, sunbathing, and enjoying water sports. However, be prepared for larger crowds and higher accommodation prices, especially in July and August when tourists flood the city. Book well in advance to secure the best accommodations.

Autumn (September to November)

Autumn brings a gentle breeze to Marseille, and the weather remains pleasant well into October. September is a fantastic time to visit, as the sea is still warm from the summer months and the beaches are less crowded. Additionally, the city's cultural scene flourishes in the autumn, with numerous festivals and events celebrating art, music, and food. During this time, you can experience the city like a local, savoring its authenticity without the summer crowds.

Winter (December to February)

While winter is the off-season for tourism, Marseille still holds its own unique appeal during this time. The city takes on a quieter, more intimate atmosphere, and you can explore museums, historic sites, and local cafes at your own pace. Winter temperatures are mild compared to many other European destinations, making it an excellent choice for travelers seeking a milder winter getaway. Christmas markets and festive lights add a touch of magic to the city's streets, making it an enchanting experience for those who embrace the winter charm.

How to Get to Marseille

Dear traveler, let me take you by the hand and lead you on an intimate journey to Marseille, unveiling the secrets of how to reach this captivating destination. Picture yourself embarking on an adventure where the path to Marseille is as enchanting as the city itself.

If you crave the magic of flying, then look no further than Marseille Provence Airport. Nestled amidst the picturesque Provençal landscapes, this modern gateway welcomes you with open arms. As you land, the anticipation builds, knowing that you're about to step into a world where history, culture, and the Mediterranean breeze converge.

Now imagine stepping onto a train, the rhythmic clacking of the wheels guiding you towards Marseille. The French countryside unfurls before your eyes, revealing rolling vineyards, charming villages, and ancient chateaux that stand like silent witnesses to the passage of time. The journey is not just a means to an end but an experience in itself, where each passing moment whispers tales of the past.

If a road trip is your heart's desire, then winding scenic routes await your arrival. As you drive, the scent of lavender dances through the air, and the landscapes change hues from lush green to golden ochre. The journey is a tapestry of panoramic vistas, a kaleidoscope of colors, and the freedom to pause wherever your heart desires. Perhaps a stop at an idyllic roadside cafe to savor a croissant and coffee, or a moment to explore a charming village perched on a hill, offering a glimpse of authentic French life

For those who crave the sea's embrace, a ferry voyage awaits. Imagine yourself sailing across the azure Mediterranean waters, the gentle sway of the waves lulling you into a state of blissful relaxation. As the shoreline of Marseille comes into view, you catch your first glimpse of the iconic Basilique Notre-Dame de la Garde, a majestic sentinel that stands tall, welcoming you to the city with its outstretched arms.

No matter which path you choose, Marseille's warmth envelops you from the moment you set foot in the city. The locals, with their friendly smiles and welcoming demeanor, make you feel like you belong here. They share their favorite spots, hidden gems, and time-honored traditions, creating an intimacy that transcends the role of a traveler.

Public Transportation in Marseille

Come, let's embark on an intimate exploration of Marseille's beating heart—the city's vibrant and accessible public transportation system. As you step onto the trams and buses, you'll feel an immediate connection to the pulse of Marseille, where locals and visitors coexist in harmony, sharing moments of everyday life.

The tramways, with their sleek and modern design, whisk you away through the city streets, revealing the tapestry of Marseille's neighborhoods. Each ride becomes a window into the soul of the city, offering glimpses of life's simple pleasures—children playing in parks, bustling street markets, and the laughter of friends sharing stories over a leisurely meal.

As you hop on a bus, you become one with the rhythm of Marseille, where time seems to slow down as you journey through its lively thoroughfares. It's a journey of togetherness as you sit shoulder-to-shoulder with locals, their warm smiles and animated conversations inviting you into their world. The bus becomes a communal space where the boundaries between strangers blur and camaraderie blooms.

Marseille's public transportation is not just a means of getting from point A to point B; it's an invitation to delve into the city's diverse soul. Each route holds its own secrets—like the hidden gem of a local café tucked away in a quaint alley, where you can savor an espresso and engage in spirited conversations with newfound friends.

As you traverse the city, the mosaic of cultures comes alive, and the multi-faceted spirit of Marseille embraces you. Arabic, French, and other languages intertwine like a harmonious melody, reminding you that Marseille is a place where cultures collide, coalesce, and celebrate one another.

And when the sun begins to set, Marseille's public transportation becomes a vessel for a captivating nocturnal voyage. The city's nightlife beckons, and trams and buses transform into vessels of shared excitement, ferrying you to vibrant bars, charming bistros, and music-filled squares where laughter and joy reign supreme.

Throughout your journeys, you'll find a deep sense of ease and accessibility. Marseille's public transportation embraces you like an old friend, guiding you effortlessly through the city's labyrinthine streets. It empowers you to discover Marseille at your own pace, inviting you to linger in places that resonate with your soul and beckoning you to explore further.

Hotel and accommodations in Marseille

My dear traveler, let's delve into the realm of accommodations in Marseille—the places that become your home away from home, where comfort and hospitality intertwine to create an unforgettable stay.

In this enchanting city, you'll find a delightful array of hotels, boutique guesthouses, and charming bed and breakfasts, each offering its own unique embrace. Picture yourself stepping into the lobby of a quaint family-run inn, where the warmth of a genuine smile greets you, instantly making you feel like an old friend returning.

As you settle into your room, the inviting ambiance envelops you—a cocoon of tranquility amidst the vibrant city. The décor reflects the essence of Marseille—colors reminiscent of the sea, artwork capturing the spirit of the Mediterranean, and touches of local craftsmanship that celebrate the city's rich cultural heritage.

From your window, you catch a glimpse of Marseille's soul—cobblestone streets winding through historic neighborhoods, the glimmering sea stretching towards the horizon, and the mesmerizing Basilique Notre-Dame de la Garde watching over the city like a benevolent guardian.

If you seek a luxurious escape, Marseille's five-star hotels are waiting to pamper you. Imagine indulging in a sumptuous spa treatment, savoring gastronomic delights crafted by talented chefs, and sipping on a glass of exquisite wine, all while enjoying breathtaking views of the city's iconic landmarks.

But perhaps you're drawn to the charm of the lesser-known, where boutique hotels become a canvas of creativity. Each room is a unique work of art, designed with passion and thoughtfulness, reflecting the spirit of Marseille's diverse neighborhoods. Here, you'll feel like a treasured guest rather than just a visitor passing through.

As the day draws to a close, returning to your accommodation is a joyful reunion, where the staff remembers your name and shares stories of the city's hidden gems. Their local insights become your guiding light, leading you to tucked-away restaurants, lively markets, and off-the-beaten-path experiences that leave a lasting imprint on your heart.

Marseille's accommodations are not just places to rest your head; they are sanctuaries of intimacy, where your journey weaves with the fabric of the city. Each morning, you awake with a sense of anticipation, knowing that the day ahead holds new discoveries, and each night, you return to the comfort of a welcoming embrace.

Hotels in Marseille

1. Ibis Marseille Centre Euromed

Address: Address: Chem. de la Haute Bédoule, 13240 Septèmes-les-Vallons, France

Phone: +33 4 91 60 99 71

Price: Starting from €70 per night

2. Lemon Hotel Plan de Campagne Marseille

Address: Chem. de la Haute Bédoule, 13240 Septèmes-les-Vallons, France

Phone: +33 4 91 60 99 71

Price: Starting from €40 per night

3. Massilia Hôtel

Address: 59 Rue des Dominicaines, 13001 Marseille, France

Phone: +33 9 80 44 96 80

Price: Starting from €50 per night

4. Mama Shelter Marseille

Address: 64 Rue de la Loubière, 13006 Marseille, France

Phone: +33 4 84 35 20 00

Price: Starting from €80 per night

5. Hôtel Belle-Vue Vieux Port

Address: 34 Quai du Port, 13002 Marseille, France

Phone: +33 4 96 17 05 40

Price: Starting from €100 per night

6. Novotel Suites Marseille Centre Euromed

Address: 33 Bd de Dunkerque, 13002 Marseille, France

Phone: +33 4 91 01 56 50

Price: Starting from €120 per night

7. Sofitel Marseille Vieux-Port

Address: 36 Bd Charles Livon, 13007 Marseille, France

Phone: +33 4 91 15 59 00

Price: Starting from €150 per night

8. Grand Hotel Beauvau Marseille Vieux-Port - MGallery

Address: 4 Rue Beauvau, 13001 Marseille, France

Phone: +33 4 91 54 91 00

Price: Starting from €200 per night

9. Mercure Marseille Centre Prado Vélodrome

Address: 11 Av. de Mazargues, 13008 Marseille, France

Phone: +33 4 96 20 37 37

Price: Starting from €130 per night

10.NH Collection Marseille

Address: Address: 37 Bd des Dames, 13002 Marseille, France

Phone: +33 4 96 11 31 20

Price: Starting from €140 per night

Chapter 2: Marseille for First-Timers

Top Attractions for First-Time Visitors

For first-time visitors to Marseille, the city offers a delightful array of attractions that embody its rich history, vibrant culture, and stunning natural beauty.

Basilique Notre-Dame de la Garde

Let me take you on a heartfelt journey to a place of profound spiritual significance—Basilique Notre-Dame de la Garde. As we ascend the hill, our spirits rise with anticipation, for we know that we are about to experience something truly extraordinary.

High above the rooftops of Marseille, the basilica stands like a guardian angel, watching over the city with a sense of unwavering devotion. Its golden statue of the Virgin Mary extends her loving arms, offering solace and protection to all who seek her embrace.

As we step inside the basilica, we are greeted by an atmosphere of serenity and reverence. The soft glow of candles casts flickering shadows on the walls, and the scent of incense hangs in the air—a gentle reminder of the prayers and aspirations whispered in this sacred space throughout the ages.

Our eyes are drawn to the breathtaking mosaics that adorn the walls and ceilings. Each tiny tile is a labor of love, forming intricate images that tell stories of faith, hope, and the enduring spirit of Marseille. The colors shimmer and dance, as if reflecting the collective spirit of the city itself—a vibrant tapestry woven with the threads of tradition and belief.

From the panoramic terrace, the city unfolds before us like a living canvas. The Vieux Port stretches out like a glistening jewel, framed by the azure waters of the Mediterranean. The bustling streets and historic landmarks below remind us that Marseille's heart beats with a timeless rhythm—a city that has weathered the tides of history and emerged with a sense of resilience and pride.

As we linger on the terrace, the sun begins to set, painting the sky with hues of pink and gold. We stand in awe of this celestial spectacle, feeling a sense of oneness with the universe, as if time itself stands still in this sacred space.

In the tranquility of the Basilique Notre-Dame de la Garde, we find a moment of inner reflection—a chance to connect with our deepest selves and the divine. It is a place where worries seem to fade away and the weight of the world is lifted from our shoulders.

As we descend from the hill, we carry the spirit of the basilica with us—a reminder of the enduring power of faith and the beauty of finding solace in the embrace of something greater than ourselves.

Basilique Notre-Dame de la Garde is more than just a place of worship; it is a sanctuary of the soul—a beacon of hope and a symbol of Marseille's unwavering spirit. It is a place where our hearts find peace and our spirits find solace—a testament to the power of faith and the intimate connection between the earthly and the divine.

Vieux Port (Old Port)

My cherished friend, let me weave a tale of enchantment as we set foot upon the historic cobblestones of Vieux Port—the beating heart of Marseille. This storied waterfront is a haven of tales, a symphony of sights and sounds that resonate with the echoes of centuries past.

As we approach the Vieux Port, the rhythmic melody of clinking boat riggings serenades us, accompanied by the harmonious chatter of seagulls soaring above. The scent of saltwater and fresh seafood fills the air, an intoxicating blend that awakens our senses to the maritime soul of the city.

Here, colorful fishing boats and elegant yachts nestle side by side, bearing witness to the city's ever-evolving spirit. The sea, a constant companion, breathes life into Marseille, forging an unbreakable bond between the people and the waters that have shaped their destiny.

The quays are lined with lively cafes and bustling markets, where the warmth of a café au lait and the indulgence of a buttery croissant offer a taste of simple pleasures. The locals—

Marseillais, with their radiant smiles—welcome us as if we were old friends, their sense of hospitality embracing us like a cherished embrace.

Stroll along the water's edge, and you'll encounter street performers and artisans, each adding their unique note to the symphony of life. The melodies of musicians, the vibrant colors of painters' palettes, and the skillful hands of craftsmen create a vibrant tableau—a reflection of Marseille's artistic spirit.

In the evening, the atmosphere takes on a magical glow as the sun dips below the horizon, painting the sky with hues of tangerine and lavender. The flickering lights of the city illuminate the waterfront, casting a dreamlike aura over the scene.

As the night unfolds, the Vieux Port transforms into a lively gathering place where laughter and music fill the air. Savor the flavors of freshly caught seafood, sip on a glass of local wine, and allow yourself to be swept away by the revelry of the moment.

At the water's edge, the lights of the Basilique Notre-Dame de la Garde glisten like a guiding star, reminding us of the spiritual presence that watches over Marseille—the guardian of its faith and resilience.

The Vieux Port is more than just a historic harbor; it is a tapestry of life—a living ode to Marseille's maritime legacy, a stage where the city's vibrant soul takes center stage. Embrace its warmth, immerse yourself in its stories, and let the rhythm of the Vieux Port's heartbeats intertwine with your own.

MuCEM (Museum of European and Mediterranean Civilizations)

My dear fellow adventurer, let us embark on a captivating journey through the corridors of time and culture as we step into the embrace of MuCEM—the Museum of European and Mediterranean Civilizations—a place where the stories of past and present merge into a harmonious tapestry.

As we approach the museum, its modern architectural brilliance stands in stark contrast to the ancient Fort Saint-Jean that it embraces—a poignant reminder of Marseille's rich history and its ever-evolving spirit. The bridge connecting the two structures is a symbolic link, a passage that bridges the gaps between the past and the present, inviting us to explore the depths of the Mediterranean's cultural heritage.

As we step inside, we are greeted by a seamless blend of light and shadow, as if the very essence of the Mediterranean has found its way into the museum's soul. The gentle murmur of visitors from around the world, speaking in various tongues, creates an ambient symphony, a testament to the diversity and unity of the Mediterranean's civilizations.

MuCEM's exhibits are a treasure trove of human stories—a tribute to the shared experiences that have shaped the cultural mosaic of the Mediterranean. Ancient artifacts and relics paint a vivid picture of the civilizations that once thrived along the shores of this legendary sea. Each piece bears witness to the dreams, triumphs, and struggles of those who walked these lands long ago.

But the museum does not dwell solely in the past; it embraces the present with equal fervor. Contemporary works of art and thought-provoking exhibits illuminate the challenges and aspirations of the Mediterranean's modern societies. Here, the spirit of innovation meets the legacy of tradition, inspiring us to reflect on our place in the grand tapestry of human existence.

As we wander through the exhibits, we find ourselves drawn to the panoramic views of the Mediterranean beyond. The sea, with its timeless expanse, seems to whisper the tales of countless journeys, trade routes, and cultural exchanges that have shaped the destiny of the region.

Outside, the MuCEM Esplanade beckons us to pause and absorb the serenity of the Mediterranean breeze. We sit amidst the shadows of the museum's sleek architecture, contemplating the interconnectedness of the human experience—our shared struggles, our shared joys, and our shared hopes for a better tomorrow.

MuCEM is more than just a museum—it is a bridge between worlds, a portal to the heart of the Mediterranean's soul. It invites us to celebrate our shared heritage, to revel in the beauty of our diversity, and to embrace the human journey with all its complexities and triumphs. As we leave MuCEM behind, may the echoes of its stories resonate within us, enriching our own understanding of the world and igniting the flame of curiosity that will forever guide us on our path of exploration.

Le Panier

Let us wander through the captivating labyrinth of Le Panier—a neighborhood that breathes life into Marseille's ancient streets, where the past merges seamlessly with the present and the artistic spirit dances freely.

As we step into Le Panier, the charm of centuries past envelops us, evident in the narrow, winding streets lined with colorful facades and charming shutters. Each step we take is a journey through time, as if the echoes of generations past whisper secrets of Marseille's storied history.

The scent of freshly baked baguettes and the gentle aroma of lavender drift from local bakeries and shops, enticing us to explore the hidden corners of this bohemian quarter. Le

Panier is a treasure trove of creativity, adorned with vibrant street art that adorns the walls like a gallery without walls.

Local artisans, with their skillful hands, showcase their crafts in quaint boutiques, where handmade trinkets and unique souvenirs await. It's a place where art is not just something you view but something you feel—an intimate encounter with the soul of Marseille's creative heartbeat.

In Le Panier's cozy squares, the gentle laughter of locals fills the air as they gather to share stories and laughter over a glass of wine or a game of pétanque. It's a place where neighbors become friends and strangers become kindred spirits, united by the enchantment of the quarter.

As we ascend to the Vieille Charité, a striking architectural gem within Le Panier, we find ourselves in awe of its grandeur—a former almshouse and a testament to the city's compassion for its people. Today, it houses museums and exhibits that celebrate art and history, providing a glimpse into Marseille's soul.

From the terraces, we catch glimpses of Marseille's rooftops and the Mediterranean beyond, where the sea beckons us to explore its mysteries. It's as if the rooftops of Le Panier offer a connection to the vast expanse of the city's spirit—a reminder that we are but a small part of a larger tapestry.

In the evening, Le Panier's narrow streets come alive with a bohemian ambiance. Cafés and restaurants spill out onto the cobblestones, creating a vibrant energy that beckons us to savor the culinary delights and bask in the joyous atmosphere.

Calanques National Park

My dear fellow adventurer, let us venture into the untamed beauty of Calanques National Park—an exquisite sanctuary where nature weaves a breathtaking tapestry of limestone cliffs, crystal-clear waters, and unspoiled wilderness.

As we approach the park, a sense of wonder washes over us, and our hearts quicken with anticipation. The Mediterranean Sea sparkles like a million diamonds, stretching out before us on a vast canvas of turquoise and cerulean.

We embark on a boat tour, and the sea breeze caresses our cheeks, carrying with it the scent of saltwater—a reminder that we are about to embark on a journey of discovery. The boat glides gracefully through the pristine waters, revealing the marvels of the Calanques—ancient fjord-like inlets carved by time and tide.

As we approach the limestone cliffs, they rise majestically from the sea, standing tall and proud, as if guardians of this natural wonder. Their rugged beauty is an ode to the passage of time—a testimony to the enduring spirit of nature.

The boat ventures into one of the coves, and we are spellbound by the sheer magnificence of the surroundings. The water, so clear and inviting, tempts us to dive in, and we lose ourselves in the embrace of the Mediterranean—a moment of pure bliss in nature's sanctuary.

On the shore, we set foot on unspoiled beaches, their soft sand a gentle caress beneath our feet. Seabirds soar overhead, their graceful flight adding to the symphony of nature's serenade. It's as if time stands still in this oasis of tranquility.

We embark on a hiking trail, and the natural world envelops us. The scent of pine trees fills the air, and the rugged terrain challenges us, rewarding us with breathtaking views at every turn. Each step is a communion with nature—a chance to reconnect with the earth and rediscover our place within the grand tapestry of life.

From the cliff edges, we gaze out over the vast expanse of the Mediterranean, feeling a profound sense of awe and humility. The Calanques are a reminder of the majesty and resilience of nature—a place where the elements have carved a masterpiece, inviting us to contemplate the wonders of creation.

As the sun begins its descent, we return to the boat, our hearts full of gratitude for this intimate encounter with the Calanques. The journey back to civilization is bittersweet, as we know that we are leaving behind a place of unparalleled beauty.

Château d'If and Frioul Archipelago

Let us set sail on an enchanting voyage to the Château d'If and the Frioul Archipelago—an adventure that will transport us to a realm of history, mystery, and breathtaking beauty.

As our boat glides across the sparkling waters of the Mediterranean, the Frioul Archipelago comes into view like a scattering of precious gems adorning the sea. The islands, each with its own unique charm, beckon us to explore their hidden treasures.

Our first destination is the iconic Château d'If, perched dramatically on a rocky islet. This historic fortress has stood the test of time, witnessing tales of incarceration and intrigue that have inspired literature and captivated the imagination of many. As we approach, the castle's imposing walls evoke a sense of awe and curiosity, as if they hold the secrets of a bygone era.

As we step onto the island, the haunting whispers of history seem to echo in the sea breeze. We explore the labyrinthine halls and dungeons, imagining the lives of the prisoners who once languished within these walls. From the rooftop terrace, the panoramic views of the Mediterranean and the distant city of Marseille offer a moment of quiet reflection—a chance to marvel at the natural beauty that surrounds this formidable fortress.

Leaving Château d'If behind, we sail towards the other islands of the Frioul Archipelago, each one a unique chapter in our maritime adventure. Ratonneau enchants us with its unspoiled beaches and idyllic coves, inviting us to bask in the embrace of the sun and sea.

On the island of Pomègues, we find a haven for wildlife and nature enthusiasts. The island's untamed beauty is a sanctuary for seabirds, and its rugged terrain offers opportunities for hiking and exploration. We lose ourselves in the sounds of nature—the lapping of waves, the rustling of leaves, and the calls of birds soaring overhead.

As the day unfolds, we pause for a leisurely lunch, savoring the flavors of the Mediterranean at one of the island's charming restaurants. The cuisine, inspired by the sea and the land, is a delight for the senses—a celebration of the bounty that surrounds us.

In the afternoon, we venture to the island of If's little sister—If Castellet. This tiny islet is a hidden gem, an intimate escape from the world. We revel in the solitude, feeling as though we've discovered a secret paradise just for us.

As the sun begins to set, we bid farewell to the Frioul Archipelago, our hearts filled with the magic of our maritime journey. The boat ride back to Marseille is a chance to reflect on the day's adventures—to treasure the moments spent exploring history, nature, and the boundless beauty of the Mediterranean.

La Corniche

My dear adventurer, let us take a leisurely stroll along the captivating coastal road of La Corniche—a picturesque promenade that hugs the Mediterranean's azure waters, offering a symphony of beauty that will surely leave a lasting impression.

As we set foot upon La Corniche, the salty sea breeze envelops us like a gentle caress, instantly awakening our senses. The sound of waves lapping against the rocky shore creates a soothing melody that accompanies our every step. With each passing moment, we feel a profound connection to the sea—a reminder of the eternal dance between land and water.

The road meanders along the coastline, revealing charming beaches and inviting coves that beckon us to linger and bask in the sun's warm embrace. The turquoise waters, like a siren's call, invite us to take a dip, to immerse ourselves in the rejuvenating sea, and to wash away the cares of the world.

As we walk, the views of Marseille's iconic landmarks come into sight—Basilique Notre-

Dame de la Garde perched high above the city and the imposing Fort Saint-Nicolas standing guard over the Old Port. These timeless symbols of Marseille's spirit add a touch of grandeur to the already magnificent scenery.

The charm of La Corniche lies not only in its natural beauty but also in the delightful amenities that dot the promenade. Charming cafes and bistros invite us to indulge in a leisurely lunch, savoring the flavors of the sea and the land. We toast to the simple joys of life—the beauty of the Mediterranean, the pleasure of good company, and the art of savoring the present moment.

As the afternoon sun bathes the coast in a golden glow, we find ourselves drawn to the viewpoints that offer panoramic vistas of the sea and the city. Here, we witness the ebb and flow of life—a never-ending dance of people and nature, each embracing the other in perfect harmony.

As the day gently transitions into evening, La Corniche takes on a magical allure. The twinkling lights of the city begin to illuminate the waterfront, creating a dreamlike ambiance. The beauty of Marseille shines brightly, a beacon that guides us back to the heart of the city, where the adventures of the day will find their continuation.

Fort Saint-Jean and the MuCEM Esplanade

Let us step into the embrace of history and culture as we explore Fort Saint-Jean and the MuCEM Esplanade—a harmonious fusion of the past and the present that invites us to immerse ourselves in Marseille's rich heritage.

As we approach Fort Saint-Jean, its sturdy stone walls stand tall, bearing witness to centuries of maritime history. The drawbridge, now a relic of the past, is a reminder of a time when the fort defended the city's entrance, safeguarding its people from the perils of the sea.

Stepping inside the fort, we find ourselves traversing the very grounds where soldiers once stood guard, and the sea breeze whispers the tales of battles and triumphs that unfolded within these walls. The courtyards and chambers, now transformed into artful spaces, invite us to contemplate the interplay of time and transformation.

Venturing further, we find ourselves on the MuCEM Esplanade—a modern architectural marvel that seems to rise effortlessly from the historic grounds of Fort Saint-Jean. The sleek lines of the museum's structure harmonize with the fort's weathered walls, as if bridging the gap between past and present.

The MuCEM Esplanade, with its open expanse, becomes a canvas for human interaction—a place where visitors from near and far gather, their diverse languages and cultures blending into a symphony of unity. The Mediterranean Sea, shimmering in the background, is a reminder of the shared heritage that binds the people of this region.

We find a moment of serenity as we sit on the esplanade, savoring the panoramic views of the Vieux Port and the bustling city beyond. The sea, with its endless horizon, beckons us to contemplate the infinite possibilities of life—a moment of introspection in the midst of vibrant activity.

As we explore the MuCEM, we are captivated by the museum's thought-provoking exhibits—celebrations of European and Mediterranean civilizations that have shaped the course of human history. Here, the past comes alive through art and artifacts, and the spirit of inquiry is ignited, inviting us to contemplate our place within the grand tapestry of human existence.

As the day gently transitions into evening, we find ourselves once again on the MuCEM Esplanade, where the setting sun paints the sky with hues of gold and pink. The view takes on a dreamlike quality, as if the past and the present blend seamlessly in the soft embrace of twilight.

Palais Longchamp

My dear adventurer, let us venture into the grandeur of Palais Longchamp—a majestic architectural masterpiece that stands as a testament to Marseille's cultural legacy and the celebration of its artistic soul.

As we approach the Palais Longchamp, its magnificent facade comes into view—a symphony of intricate details and stately columns that exude a sense of grandeur. The palace's presence is awe-inspiring, a reminder of the city's reverence for art and beauty.

We step inside, and the spacious halls beckon us to explore their opulence. The echoes of history seem to reverberate within these walls, as if the past has left its mark on every inch of the building. Here, we find the Museum of Fine Arts and the Museum of Natural History—a treasure trove of artistic wonders and scientific discoveries.

In the Museum of Fine Arts, masterpieces by renowned artists from different eras grace the walls. Paintings and sculptures tell stories of human emotions, passion, and creativity—a timeless connection between the artist and the observer. The museum's collection is a testament to Marseille's appreciation for art—a city that has nurtured talent and embraced artistic expression throughout the ages.

In the Museum of Natural History, we embark on a journey through the wonders of the natural world. Here, we encounter fossils of ancient creatures, scientific discoveries that spark our curiosity, and exhibits that celebrate the beauty and diversity of life. The museum is a tribute to the natural wonders that surround us—a reminder of our responsibility to protect and cherish the environment.

Beyond the walls of the palace lies a verdant oasis—the Parc Longchamp—a sprawling garden adorned with lush greenery, statues, and fountains. The central fountain, with its cascading waters and sculpted figures, is a mesmerizing sight that beckons us to pause and marvel at the beauty of human ingenuity and artistry.

As we wander through the park, the fragrance of blooming flowers fills the air, and the sound of laughter and the playful footsteps of children add to the park's joyous atmosphere. Palais Longchamp and its surrounding gardens are not just a place to visit; they are a place to be, to find tranquility, and to appreciate the harmony of art and nature.

In the twilight hours, the palace and its gardens take on a magical aura. The soft glow of the lights illuminates the grandeur of the architecture, creating a captivating ambiance that is nothing short of enchanting.

Cours Julien

Let us immerse ourselves in the bohemian spirit of Cours Julien—a vibrant neighborhood in Marseille that pulsates with creativity, where art, culture, and a sense of community thrive in perfect harmony.

As we step into Cours Julien, a kaleidoscope of colors greets us at every turn. Street art adorns the walls, breathing life into the streets, while graffiti artists add their own artistic expressions to the urban canvas. Each stroke of paint is a glimpse into the soul of Marseille, a city that embraces creativity as an essential part of its identity.

The atmosphere is electric, with a palpable sense of freedom and artistic energy lingering in the air. Local musicians strum their guitars, their melodies blending with the laughter and chatter of residents and visitors alike. Cours Julien is not just a place—it's a state of mind, a celebration of individuality, and an homage to the creative spirit.

The neighborhood's squares are a delightful chaos of activity, with open-air markets offering an array of artisanal goods, vintage treasures, and handmade crafts. Here, we find ourselves drawn to the unique and the unconventional, as Cours Julien encourages us to embrace our quirks and appreciate the beauty of the unconventional.

Charming cafes and cozy bistros invite us to take a seat and savor the eclectic flavors of Marseille's culinary scene. The cuisine here is a fusion of cultures—a reflection of the diverse influences that have shaped the city's gastronomic identity.

As we explore the labyrinthine streets, we stumble upon hidden boutiques and art galleries where local artists display their creations with pride. The vibrant art scene is an invitation to explore the world through the eyes of the artist—to see beauty in the mundane and find inspiration in the ordinary.

At nightfall, Cours Julien transforms into a lively hub of nightlife. Music spills out from bars, and the clinking of glasses accompanies the vivacious conversations of patrons enjoying the ambiance of the evening. The night is young, and the spirit of camaraderie and artistic expression fills the air.

Cours Julien is more than just a neighborhood—it is a sanctuary for the free-spirited, a refuge for the creative soul, and a testament to Marseille's unyielding commitment to artistic freedom. Here, in the heart of the city, we find a haven of self-expression, a place where individuality is celebrated and the boundaries of art are constantly pushed.

Where to Stay in Marseille: A Neighborhood Guide

My dear friend, let me be your personal guide as we embark on a heartfelt exploration of the enchanting neighborhoods of Marseille—a city that offers a kaleidoscope of experiences, each one inviting you to immerse yourself in its unique charm and spirit.

Vieux Port (Old Port)

At the heart of Marseille's soul, the Vieux Port is a lively and historic neighborhood that beckons you to stay amidst the hustle and bustle of the city's maritime heart. Choose a charming boutique hotel or a quaint guesthouse along the quays, and wake up to the sight of colorful fishing boats gently swaying in the water. Here, you'll be immersed in the vibrant energy of the city, with a plethora of restaurants, cafes, and shops at your doorstep.

Le Panier

For those seeking a bohemian and artistic experience, Le Panier is a haven of creativity and charm. Stay in a cozy Airbnb or a boutique hotel tucked away in its narrow streets, where colorful street art adorns the walls and hidden squares invite you to explore. Le Panier is a neighborhood that embraces individuality, and you'll find yourself immersed in its vibrant and eclectic atmosphere.

La Corniche

If tranquility and stunning views are what you seek, La Corniche is the perfect choice. Perched along the coastal road, this neighborhood offers luxurious hotels and boutique accommodations with breathtaking vistas of the Mediterranean. Wake up to the soothing sound of waves and indulge in leisurely walks along the scenic promenade. La Corniche is a place to find solace and relaxation while still being within reach of Marseille's bustling heart.

Endoume

For a more residential and authentic experience, consider staying in Endoume, a charming neighborhood with a local flair. Here, you'll find quaint bed and breakfasts and family-run guesthouses, allowing you to immerse yourself in the daily lives of Marseille's residents. Enjoy leisurely strolls to nearby markets and parks, and savor the simple pleasures of life in this inviting and friendly neighborhood.

Le Prado

If you desire a beachside retreat, Le Prado is the ideal destination. Stay in one of the upscale hotels or elegant beachfront resorts, where you can wake up to the sound of seagulls and the scent of the sea. Enjoy leisurely days on the sandy shores or take a relaxing walk along the palm-lined promenade. Le Prado offers a perfect blend of relaxation and accessibility to the city's attractions.

Essential French Phrases for Travelers

As you embark on your journey to the enchanting land of France, let me be your companion in preparing for an immersive and authentic experience. Embrace the beauty of the French language, and let these essential phrases become the key that unlocks the hearts of the locals and allows you to connect with the soul of the country.

Greetings

- Bonjour (bohn-zhoor): "Hello"
- Salut (sah-lyoo): "Hi"
- Bonsoir (bohn-swahr): "Good evening."
- Coucou (koo-koo): "Hey" (informal and friendly)

Ordering Food and Drinks

- Je voudrais... (zhuh voo-dreh): "I would like..."
- L'addition, s'il vous plaît (lah-dee-syon, seel voo pleh): "The bill, please."
- Un café, s'il vous plaît (uhn kah-fay, seel voo pleh): "A coffee, please."
- Une baguette, s'il vous plaît (ewn bah-get, seel voo pleh): "A baguette, please"

Polite Expressions

- Merci (mehr-see): "Thank you"
- De rien (duh ryehn): "You're welcome."
- Excusez-moi (ex-kew-zay mwah): "Excuse me."
- Pardon (par-dohn): "Sorry" or "Pardon me."

Basic Communication

- Oui (wee): "Yes"
- Non (nohn): "No"
- Parlez-vous anglais? (par-leh voo zon-gleh): "Do you speak English?"
- Je ne parle pas français (zhuh nuh parl pah frahn-seh): "I don't speak French."

Asking for Help

- Pouvez-vous m'aider, s'il vous plaît? (poo-vez voo may-day, seel voo pleh): "Can you help me, please?"
- Je suis perdue (zhuh swee pehr-doo): "I am lost."
- Je cherche... (zhuh shehrsh): "I am looking for..."

Directions

- Oùest...? (oo eh): "Where is...?"

- À gauche (ah gohsh): "To the left"
- À droite (ah drwah): "To the right"
- Tout droit (toot drwah): "Straight ahead"

Time

- Quelle heure est-il ? (kehl er eh-teel) - "What time is it?"
- Il est... (eel eh) - "It is..."
- Le matin (luh ma-tahn) - "Morning"
- L'après-midi (lah-preh-mee-dee): "Afternoon"

Safety Tips and Precautions

My dear friend, as you embark on your journey to Marseille, your safety and well-being are of utmost importance to me. Let me share some intimate safety tips and precautions to ensure that your experience in this captivating city is filled with joy, comfort, and peace of mind.

1. **Stay Aware of Your surroundings**: Marseille is a vibrant and bustling city, and like any other urban destination, it's essential to remain aware of your surroundings. Be mindful of your belongings, especially in crowded areas and on public transportation. A secure cross-body bag or a money belt can be helpful to keep your valuables safe.

2. **Trust Your Instincts**: Your intuition is a powerful ally. If you ever feel uncomfortable or uncertain about a situation or place, trust your gut and remove yourself from it. It's always better to err on the side of caution.

3. **Avoid Dark and Secluded Areas at night**: While Marseille is generally safe, it's advisable to avoid poorly lit and isolated areas, particularly at night. Stick to well-populated streets and well-known neighborhoods to ensure your safety.

4. **Learn Some Basic French Phrases**: Knowing a few basic French phrases can go a long way toward making your journey smoother and safer. Locals

appreciate the effort, and it can help you navigate situations with ease.

5. **Use Official Transportation Services**: When taking taxis or rideshare services, opt for official and licensed providers. Be cautious about accepting rides from unmarked or unofficial vehicles.

Chapter 3: Marseille Travel Itinerary

Unveiling Marseille: A 3-Day Voyage through Mediterranean Magic

Step into a realm where azure skies meet turquoise waters, where ancient history blends seamlessly with vibrant modernity, and where the essence of Provence infuses every corner with its aromatic charm. Welcome to Marseille, a city that beckons adventurers with its intoxicating blend of culture, nature, and culinary delights. Embark on a journey that will lead you from the heights of basilicas to the depths of calanques, from bustling ports to hidden alleyways steeped in history.

Day 1: Captivating Heights and Harbor Charms

Prepare for an awe-inspiring ascent as you venture to the iconic Basilique Notre-Dame de la Garde. The morning sun casts a golden glow on the city as you take in sweeping vistas that stretch to the horizon. Wander down to the historic Vieux Port (Old Port), where the symphony of clinking glasses and seafaring tales beckon. Here, you'll taste the heart and soul of Marseille through its seafood delicacies.

In the afternoon, the enchantment of Le Panier district unfolds before you. Cobblestone streets wind through a canvas of pastel facades, charming boutiques, and art studios that breathe life into Marseille's artistic soul. As the sun dips toward the sea, embark on a leisurely journey along La Corniche—a coastal path where the Mediterranean's gentle waves whisper tales of ancient mariners.

Day 2: A Cultural Sojourn and Secrets Unveiled

Awaken your curiosity at the MuCEM (Museum of European and Mediterranean Civilizations), a modern masterpiece that bridges the past and present. Wander the fortifications of Fort Saint-Jean, where history unfolds amidst architectural grandeur and panoramic views. The majestic Cathédrale de la Major awaits, adorned with stories of devotion and architectural splendor.

As dusk descends, wander back through the maze-like alleys of Le Panier, where history echoes through every stone. Indulge in a culinary journey that tantalizes the senses with Provençal flavors, setting the stage for an evening of local music and artistic performances.

Day 3: Nature's Embrace and Seaside Serenity

Rise early for a rendezvous with nature's masterpiece—the Calanques National Park. A boat ride unveils the majesty of rugged cliffs meeting the tranquil sea, where hidden coves and azure waters beckon swimmers and dreamers alike. Back in the heart of Marseille, the allure of Vallon des Auffes unveils itself—a picturesque fishing village where time seems to stand still.

Savor your final Provençal lunch near the shimmering Vieux Port, letting the flavors linger as you reflect on your voyage. An afternoon stroll captures the city's essence—a seamless blend of history, culture, and Mediterranean beauty. With the sunset casting its warm embrace, you bid farewell to Marseille, carrying its enchantment and memories into your journey forward.

Marseille and Beyond: A 7-Day Odyssey Through Southern Splendor

Prepare to embark on a week-long voyage that will immerse you in the treasures of Marseille and its neighboring delights. From the heights of basilicas to the depths of calanques, from charming villages to historic towns, this itinerary unfolds a tapestry of experiences that showcase the beauty and diversity of the region.

Day 1: Arrival and Marseille Introduction

- Arrive in Marseille and settle into your accommodations. Spend the afternoon exploring the iconic Vieux Port (Old Port).

- Immerse yourself in the bustling maritime atmosphere and savor a traditional Provençal dinner by the water.

Day 2: Basilicas and City Wonders

- Ascend to the Basilique Notre-Dame de la Garde to witness panoramic views of Marseille.

- Explore the historic heart of Marseille, wandering through the maze-like alleys of Le Panier district.

- Discover the historic treasures of Fort Saint-Jean and the modern architectural wonder of the MuCEM.

Day 3: Coastal Charms and Hidden Gems

- Embark on a boat tour to the Calanques National Park.

- Swim in azure waters and explore hidden coves.

- Return to the city to enjoy a relaxed evening at the charming Vallon des Auffes fishing village.

Day 4: Aix-en-Provence Day Trip

- Take a day trip to the charming town of Aix-en-Provence.

- Explore its elegant boulevards, historic architecture, and vibrant culture.

- Visit the Cours Mirabeau, the Vieil Aix (Old Town), and the stunning Saint-Sauveur Cathedral.

Day 5: Arles Exploration

- Travel to Arles to experience its ancient Roman heritage and artistic legacy.

- Visit the Amphitheatre, the Roman Theatre, and the historic Place du Forum.

- Immerse yourself in the footsteps of Vincent van Gogh with visits to key locations that inspired his art.

Day 6: Cassis and Mediterranean Bliss

- Journey to the charming coastal village of Cassis.

- Explore the Calanques by boat and enjoy the stunning scenery.

- Stroll through the picturesque harbor and savor fresh seafood by the waterfront.

Day 7: Farewell Marseille

- Spend your final day indulging in last-minute shopping or revisiting your favorite Marseille spots.

- Take a leisurely stroll along La Corniche and bid farewell to the Mediterranean's embrace.

- Enjoy a memorable final dinner at a local restaurant, savoring the flavors of Provence.

As your week-long odyssey through Marseille and its surroundings comes to an end, you carry with you a mosaic of experiences that embody the spirit of Southern France. From vibrant cities to tranquil coastal gems, this journey has revealed the diverse facets of a region that captivates with its history, culture, and natural beauty. As you depart, may the memories of this enchanting week continue to enrich your travels and inspire your future explorations.

Marseille Family Adventure: A 7-Day Journey of Discovery and Fun

Get ready for a week of family-friendly exploration and memorable moments in Marseille and its surrounding treasures. This itinerary is designed to engage travelers of all ages, combining cultural experiences, outdoor adventures, and delightful activities that the whole family can enjoy.

Day 1: Arrival and Maritime Marvels
- Arrive in Marseille and settle into your family-friendly accommodations.

- Begin your adventure at the Vieux Port (Old Port), where kids can spot colorful boats and seagulls while parents enjoy the bustling atmosphere.

- Enjoy an early dinner at a waterfront restaurant, savoring the fresh flavors of Mediterranean cuisine.

Day 2: Sea, Sun, and Panoramic Views
- Head to the Basilique Notre-Dame de la Garde for stunning panoramic views of the city. Kids will love spotting landmarks from above.

- Afternoon visit to the MuCEM, an interactive museum where kids can engage with history and culture in a playful way.

Day 3: Calanques and Coastal Magic

- Embark on a family-friendly boat tour to the Calanques National Park. Swim, snorkel, and explore hidden coves.

- Return to the city and have a relaxed dinner at the charming Vallon des Auffes, where kids can enjoy watching the fishing boats.

Day 4: Aix-en-Provence and Playful Explorations

- Take a day trip to Aix-en-Provence, known for its artistic atmosphere and vibrant markets.

- Visit the Cours Mirabeau, where kids can enjoy ice cream and street performers.

Day 5: Van Gogh's Adventure in Arles

- Travel to Arles and explore its Roman heritage.

- Kids can participate in a fun "Van Gogh Scavenger Hunt" to discover the spots that inspired the artist's famous paintings.

Day 6: Cassis and Calanques Delight

- Venture to the coastal village of Cassis.

- Kids will love the boat ride to the calanques, and parents can appreciate the stunning scenery.

- Explore the village and enjoy beach time before heading back to Marseille.

Day 7: Marseille Play and Farewell

- Spend a playful morning at the Jardin des Vestiges, an archaeological park with Roman ruins that kids can explore.

- Afternoon at the Parc Borély, where families can picnic, rent pedal boats, or simply enjoy the greenery.

- Have a joyful farewell dinner, reflecting on the amazing family memories you've created in Marseille.

As you bid Marseille adieu, your family leaves with a treasure trove of shared experiences and joyful moments. From the heights of basilicas to the depths of calanques, from historical explorations to delightful play, this family-friendly journey has woven the magic of

Marseille into the hearts of all who embarked on this adventure together.

Marseille through the Lens: A 7-Day Photography Expedition

Capture the essence of Marseille's beauty and its surrounding gems through your camera lens. This itinerary is tailored for photography enthusiasts, allowing you to capture the city's vibrant culture, historic treasures, and natural landscapes in all their glory.

Day 1: Arrival and Harbor Beginnings

- Arrive in Marseille and settle into your accommodations.

- Begin your photographic journey at the Vieux Port (Old Port), capturing the lively maritime atmosphere and the reflections of boats on the water.

Day 2: Cityscapes and Architecture

- Start the day by photographing the stunning cityscape from the Basilique Notre-Dame de la Garde.

- Explore the unique architecture of the MuCEM and Fort Saint-Jean, experimenting with different angles and compositions.

Day 3: Calanques and Coastal Magic

- Embark on a photography-focused boat tour to the Calanques National Park.

- Capture the dramatic cliffs, turquoise waters, and hidden coves.

- Return to the city and photograph the quaint charm of Vallon des Auffes.

Day 4: Aix-en-Provence in Frames
- Take a day trip to Aix-en-Provence and capture the town's elegant streets, colorful markets, and historic architecture.

- Explore the interplay of light and shadow along the Cours Mirabeau and within the bustling markets.

Day 5: Arles in Focus
- Travel to Arles and immerse yourself in its Roman heritage and artistic ambiance.

- Capture the details that inspired Van Gogh and experiment with capturing the vibrant life of the Place du Forum.

Day 6: Captivating Cassis

- Head to the coastal village of Cassis. Photograph the picturesque harbor, the rugged coastline, and the charming streets.

- Capture the calanques' breathtaking landscapes during a boat tour, focusing on the interplay of nature and water.

Day 7: Marseille Farewell in Frames

- Spend your last day revisiting your favorite Marseille spots, capturing the bustling streets and vibrant local life.

- Capture the sunset along La Corniche, capturing the changing colors of the sky against the sea.
- End your journey with a final photographic exploration of the city's

hidden corners and well-known landmarks.

As you bid farewell to Marseille, your camera is filled with moments frozen in time—captured views, artistic angles, and the essence of a city that has revealed its beauty through your lens. Carry these photographic treasures with you as you continue to explore the world through your artistry, and may the images you've captured serve as a vivid reminder of the remarkable journey you've embarked upon in Marseille.

Chapter 4: Hidden Gems in Marseille

Off-the-Beaten-Path Places to Explore

My dear adventurous friend, let's embark on a journey to uncover the hidden gems and off-the-beaten-path places that lie beyond the tourist trails of Marseille. These lesser-known treasures are waiting to be discovered, promising you a unique and intimate experience like no other.

Vallon des Auffes

Dear fellow traveler let me paint a vivid picture of Vallon des Auffes—a hidden jewel nestled along the azure waters of Marseille's coastline. Here, time seems to slow down, and the charm of a bygone era envelops you in its warm embrace.

As we approach Vallon des Auffes, the first glimpse of this picturesque fishing village takes our breath away. Colorful boats line the small harbor, gently rocking with the rhythm of the sea. The water sparkles like diamonds, inviting us to dip our toes into its cool embrace.

We meander along the narrow alleys, where quaint houses with terracotta roofs seem to lean affectionately toward one another. Bougainvillea vines cascade down the walls, their vibrant blooms adding a burst of color to the rustic scenery. Each step brings us closer to the heart of this timeless haven.

Locals go about their daily lives with a sense of tranquility, welcoming visitors with warm smiles that radiate a genuine sense of community. The fishing nets are neatly arranged, and the aroma of freshly caught seafood mingles with the salty sea breeze—a testament to the villages age-old ties to the sea.

At the heart of Vallon des Auffes, a charming row of seafood restaurants perched on the rocky shore beckons us to indulge in the flavors of the Mediterranean. Here, we savor the catch of the day, prepared with love and skill by the skilled chefs. The sound of laughter and clinking glasses creates a convivial atmosphere that invites us to linger in the moment.

As the sun begins to set, the skies above Vallon des Auffes transform into a canvas of hues—splashes of pinks, oranges, and purples that reflect upon the tranquil waters below. We find ourselves drawn to the edge of the harbor, where we sit in quiet contemplation, the beauty of this hidden gem etching itself into our hearts.

In the twilight hours, Vallon des Auffes takes on a magical aura. The lights of the fishing boats twinkle like stars on the water, and the village comes alive with an enchanting glow. It's a moment frozen in time—a place where the simplicity of life and the magnificence of nature blend seamlessly.

My dear friend, Vallon des Auffes, is more than just a fishing village—it's a sanctuary of serenity and a testament to Marseille's intimate relationship with the sea.

Les Goudes

Dear fellow traveler, let me whisk you away to the enchanting world of Les Goudes—an unspoiled haven at the edge of Marseille, where untamed beauty and the rhythm of the sea dance in harmony. Here, the spirit of adventure beckons, and the allure of nature's embrace captivates your soul.

As we venture to Les Goudes, the city's hustle slowly fades away, replaced by a sense of tranquility that envelops us like a gentle caress. The road winds along the rugged coastline, revealing glimpses of turquoise waters and rocky cliffs that stretch into the horizon.

Upon arrival, the quaint fishing village of Les Goudes welcomes us with open arms. Traditional cottages, adorned with colorful shutters, stand proudly against the backdrop of the azure Mediterranean. The scent of salty sea air fills the atmosphere, and the sound of seagulls soaring overhead adds a touch of magic to the ambiance.

Embrace the spirit of exploration as we set foot on the rugged paths that wind through the Calanques. Majestic cliffs tower above us, and the sea below sparkles like a precious gem. The serenity of nature surrounds us, and we find ourselves in awe of the raw beauty that surrounds this hidden gem.

For the adventurous at heart, hiking along the coastal trails offers breathtaking views at every turn. The Calanques beckon us to discover their secret coves and hidden beaches, inviting us to dip our toes into the refreshing waters and bask in the solitude of nature's embrace.

As the day slowly unfolds, we venture to a local tavern, where the aroma of fresh seafood fills the air. Here, we savor the catch of the day, lovingly prepared by the village's skilled fishermen. The taste of the Mediterranean delights our senses, and we share tales of our adventures with the locals, creating a sense of camaraderie that transcends language barriers.

In the embrace of twilight, Les Goudes takes on a mystical aura. The setting sun paints the sky with hues of orange and pink, casting a golden glow over the village and the sea. As night descends, the stars twinkle overhead, guiding us back to the village, where we find comfort in the simplicity of life and the beauty of a world untouched by time.

Rue de la République

Dear fellow traveler, let me lead you down the vibrant and lively Rue de la République—a bustling street that pulses with the heartbeats of Marseille's daily life. Here, the past blends seamlessly with the present, and a tapestry of history and modernity awaits your exploration.

As we step onto Rue de la République, the energy of the city envelops us like a warm embrace. This grand avenue is adorned with elegant Haussmannian buildings, their facades telling stories of a bygone era. Ornate balconies overlook the street, as if inviting us to witness the vibrant scenes that unfold below.

The rhythm of footsteps echoes through the boulevard as locals and visitors alike traverse this urban artery. A cornucopia of shops and boutiques line the street, showcasing everything from high-end fashion to local crafts—a treasure trove of discoveries awaits at every turn.

Cafés and brasseries dot the landscape, their outdoor terraces beckoning us to take a moment and indulge in the art of people-watching. The aroma of freshly brewed coffee and delicate pastries fills the air, tantalizing our senses as we soak in the lively ambiance of this grand boulevard.

As we stroll along Rue de la République, we pass historical landmarks that bear witness to Marseille's rich heritage. Glance to your left, and you'll find the historic Bourse Building, a magnificent testament to Marseille's 19th-century architectural prowess. Turn to your right, and the majestic Palais de la Bourse stands proud, a reminder of the city's economic importance.

At the heart of this vibrant street, street performers showcase their talents, filling the air with music, laughter, and applause. Their artistry adds an enchanting touch to the lively tapestry of

Rue de la République, infusing the boulevard with a sense of creative spirit.

As the sun sets, the Rue de la République comes alive with a dazzling display of lights. The grand street takes on a magical aura, and the beauty of Marseille's urban landscape is illuminated under the starry sky.

My dear friend, Rue de la République is not just a street—it's a living testament to Marseille's vibrant soul.

Cité Radieuse, Le Corbusier's Masterpiece

Dear fellow traveler let me take you on a journey to Cité Radieuse—a visionary masterpiece crafted by the renowned architect Le Corbusier, nestled amidst the vibrant cityscape of Marseille. Prepare to be enthralled by its innovative design and the artistic vision that transformed urban living into an extraordinary work of art.

As we approach Cité Radieuse, its imposing presence commands our attention. This architectural marvel rises like a vertical village, an avant-garde structure that defies conventions and embraces the ideals of modernist architecture.

As we step inside, we are welcomed into a world of harmonious living. Le Corbusier's vision comes to life through its innovative design, where functionality meets beauty and every element serves a purpose. The building is organized into self-sufficient residential units, each featuring a private balcony that offers breathtaking views of the city and the sea beyond.

The heart of Cité Radieuse is its communal spaces, where residents can come together to socialize and engage in community activities. The rooftop terrace, with its open-air gym, pool, and sundeck, becomes a sanctuary of relaxation and interaction. Here, the boundaries between private and public spaces blur, fostering a sense of unity and camaraderie among the residents.

Wandering through the corridors, we encounter a labyrinth of colors and shapes, where Le

Corbusier's signature use of primary colors and geometric forms delights the eye. The building becomes an ever-changing canvas as the interplay of light and shadows creates a captivating dance throughout the day.

Cité Radieuse is not just a building—it's a way of life. Its design aims to enhance the well-being of its residents by promoting a sense of community and shared responsibility. The thoughtful incorporation of green spaces, schools, shops, and cultural facilities further enriches the lives of those who call Cité Radieuse home.

Beyond its architectural brilliance, Cité Radieuse stands as a testament to Marseille's progressive spirit. Its construction in the post-war era symbolizes hope and renewal—a symbol of the city's resilience and determination to embrace the future.

Calanque de Sugiton

My dear friend, let me transport you to the breathtaking beauty of Calanque de Sugiton, a hidden gem nestled along the rugged coastline of Marseille. Prepare to be enchanted by the untamed splendor of nature as we venture into this pristine cove, where azure waters meet majestic limestone cliffs in perfect harmony.

As we approach Calanque de Sugiton, the sight before us takes our breath away. The crystal-clear waters of the Mediterranean sparkle like a precious gem, inviting us to immerse ourselves in their refreshing embrace. The limestone cliffs, weathered by time, stand tall and proud, providing a dramatic backdrop to this natural wonder.

The hike to Calanque de Sugiton is an adventure in itself. As we traverse the rocky paths, we're surrounded by the scents of wild herbs and the soothing sound of the sea below. With each step, anticipation builds, knowing that a hidden paradise awaits us at the end of the trail.

Finally, we reach the secluded cove, and its beauty surpasses our wildest dreams. A crescent of soft golden sand beckons us to relax and unwind, while the vibrant blue waters tempt us to take a refreshing dip. The silence is broken only by the gentle lapping of the waves against the shore, creating a sense of tranquility that envelops us like a warm embrace.

For adventurous spirits, there are countless opportunities to explore. Climb the cliffs to capture panoramic views of the Mediterranean, or venture into the inviting waters to snorkel and discover the colorful marine life that thrives beneath the surface.

As the day progresses, the sun begins its descent, casting a golden glow over Calanque de Sugiton. The play of light and shadow paints a mesmerizing portrait of nature's beauty. We find ourselves captivated by the simplicity of this hidden paradise, where the marvels of the natural world take center stage.

With a heavy heart, we bid farewell to Calanque de Sugiton, knowing that its memory will forever linger in our hearts. As we carry this treasure with us, may the serenity and splendor of this secluded cove inspire us to seek out the hidden wonders of the world and embrace the magic that lies off the beaten path.

Palais Longchamp Gardens

Dear fellow traveler, let me take you on a leisurely stroll through the enchanting Palais Longchamp Gardens—a lush oasis that lies within the heart of Marseille, offering respite from the urban bustle and a glimpse into the city's historical grandeur.

As we approach Palais Longchamp, its majestic facade comes into view—a masterpiece of neoclassical architecture that commands attention with its grandeur. Built in the 19th century, the Palais serves as a tribute to the construction of the Canal de Marseille, an engineering marvel that brought water to the city, ensuring its prosperity.

Passing through the palais, we enter the serene gardens, where a sense of tranquility washes over us. The fragrance of blooming flowers fills the air, and the gentle sound of fountains whispers of timeless elegance. A vast expanse of greenery stretches before us, inviting us to explore its hidden corners.

Amidst the well-manicured lawns and picturesque alleys, we discover charming sculptures and architectural elements that add a touch of whimsy to the landscape. Each corner seems to hold a story—a testament to the city's rich history and artistic heritage.

The central feature of the gardens is the stunning cascade—a grand waterfall that cascades down a majestic staircase. As the water glistens in the sunlight, we find ourselves mesmerized by the dance of light and shadow, a mesmerizing display that captivates our senses.

Beyond the cascade lie the Palais Longchamp's water reservoirs—massive stone basins that once served as a vital source of water for Marseille. Today, these reservoirs are adorned with beautiful water lilies and provide a serene setting for contemplation and relaxation.

Along the garden's edges, towering trees create shady alcoves, offering a tranquil escape from the warmth of the sun. We find benches nestled beneath their leafy canopies, inviting us to sit and savor the moments of blissful solitude.

As the day draws to a close, the gardens of Palais Longchamp take on a magical aura. Soft evening light bathes the landscape in a warm glow, casting a serene ambiance that feels almost otherworldly.

Vieille Charité

My dear friend, let me guide you through the storied halls of Vieille Charité, a magnificent architectural gem nestled in the heart of Marseille's historic Panier district. Prepare to be transported to a place where history, art, and compassion intertwine to create an enchanting haven of culture and humanity.

As we approach Vieille Charité, its elegant facade comes into view—a stunning testament to Baroque architecture, showcasing its grandeur with intricate details and a sense of timeless grace. Built in the 17th century, this former almshouse once offered shelter and care to the city's most vulnerable citizens.

Stepping through the entrance, we find ourselves in a tranquil courtyard—a sanctuary of serenity where lush greenery surrounds us and the soothing sound of water features fills the air. It's as if time has stood still, and the echoes of the past linger in every corner of this historic space.

The Vieille Charité is not just a building; it's a cultural complex that houses some of Marseille's most esteemed institutions. Its stunning arcades lead us to museums, galleries, and cultural spaces that celebrate the richness of art, history, and archaeology.

As we explore the museums, we are met with a vast collection of artifacts that offer a glimpse into the city's diverse past. From ancient civilizations to contemporary art, the exhibits here showcase the breadth of Marseille's cultural heritage, allowing us to walk in the footsteps of those who have shaped this city through the ages.

The chapel of Vieille Charité stands as a breathtaking testament to the building's historic significance. Adorned with beautiful frescoes and intricate carvings, the chapel invites us to pause and reflect on the spiritual importance that this place once held for the vulnerable souls who sought solace within its walls.

As we wander through the arcades and corridors, we encounter inviting courtyards that serve as gathering spaces for locals and visitors alike. These serene enclaves become oases of contemplation, inviting us to sit and absorb the beauty that surrounds us.

Beyond its architectural brilliance and cultural significance, Vieille Charité remains a beacon of compassion and human connection. Though its purpose has evolved over the centuries, its commitment to fostering a sense of community and caring for one another endures.

Îles du Frioul

My dear friend, let me whisk you away to the serene Îles du Frioul—a group of idyllic islands just off the coast of Marseille, where the beauty of nature and the allure of the Mediterranean await to enchant you.

As we board the boat to Îles du Frioul, the sea breeze caresses our faces, and the excitement of exploration fills the air. Leaving the mainland behind, we set sail towards these unspoiled paradises, where time seems to slow down and worries are left behind.

As the islands come into view, we are greeted by a postcard-worthy panorama—a tapestry of azure waters, rocky shores, and lush greenery. The islands seem to rise from the sea like guardians of tranquility, inviting us to step into their embrace.

Upon arrival, we find ourselves on the main island of Pomègues, where simplicity and natural beauty reign. The absence of cars and bustling crowds adds to the sense of serenity as we explore the island's network of hiking trails that lead us through fragrant maquis and offer panoramic views of the Mediterranean.

As we venture further, we encounter secluded coves with pristine beaches where we can bask in the sun or take a refreshing dip in the clear waters. The gentle lapping of the waves becomes a soothing symphony that lulls us into a state of pure relaxation.

Nature thrives on Îles du Frioul, and wildlife enthusiasts will find themselves in awe of the diverse birdlife that inhabits the islands. Seagulls soar overhead, while colorful migratory birds make a pitstop during their journeys—a spectacle that adds to the enchantment of this hidden sanctuary.

For history buffs, the island of Ratonneau offers a journey back in time. Here, the historic Fort de Ratonneau stands as a reminder of the islands' strategic importance in maritime defense. Exploring the fortress and its labyrinthine passages is like stepping into history, where tales of bygone eras come alive.

As the sun begins to set, we find ourselves on the Esplanade de la Tourette, a tranquil square that offers breathtaking views of the sunset over the sea. The sky transforms into a canvas of vivid colors, bidding us farewell with a spectacular display of nature's artistry.

My dear friend, the Îles du Frioul are not just islands—they are sanctuaries of serenity and natural wonder. As we bid adieu to this paradise, let the memories of its unspoiled beauty stay with us, reminding us to seek solace in nature and embrace the simplicity of life. May the magic of the Îles du Frioul linger in our hearts, inspiring us to cherish the moments of tranquility that can be found amidst the vastness of the world's wonders.

Lesser-Known Museums and Art Galleries

My dear friend, let me take you on a journey to discover the lesser-known museums and art galleries of Marseille—a treasure trove of artistic gems that lie beyond the beaten path, waiting to captivate your heart and mind.

Musée d'Histoire de Marseille (Museum of Marseille History)

My dear friend, come with me as we step back in time and immerse ourselves in the captivating world of the Musée d'Histoire de Marseille—the Museum of Marseille History. Let's embark on a journey that will bring to life the extraordinary stories and ancient wonders that have shaped this remarkable city throughout the ages.

As we approach the museum, a sense of excitement tingles in the air, knowing that we are about to unravel the layers of Marseille's past. The grand facade stands as a gateway to history, inviting us to venture inside and explore the mysteries that lie within.

The moment we step through the museum's doors, we are transported back in time. The air seems to whisper tales of ancient civilizations, and the walls hum with the echoes of past glories. Each exhibit is a doorway to a different era, and we find ourselves traveling through the ages, from the foundations of Massalia, the ancient Greek city, to the bustling port town of today.

The artifacts and archaeological findings on display bring history to life before our eyes.

Pottery from centuries past, intricate jewelry, and artifacts unearthed from ancient shipwrecks all bear witness to Marseille's storied maritime heritage. We are humbled by the sense of continuity, knowing that the same Mediterranean sea that once connected distant civilizations still embraces the shores of Marseille today.

The museum's multimedia exhibits add an immersive dimension to the experience. As we wander through the recreated streets of ancient Massalia, we can almost feel the heartbeat of the city that once flourished in these very spots. The interactive displays invite us to explore, learn, and understand the lives of the people who called this place home.

One of the highlights of the museum is the depiction of Marseille's resilience during challenging times. We witness the city's fortitude through its rebuilding after devastating fires and wars, a testament to the indomitable spirit that has always defined Marseille and its people.

As we reach the contemporary exhibits, we are reminded that history is a living tapestry, continually woven by the hands of time. The vibrancy of Marseille's present-day life is woven into the narrative, honoring the city's heritage while embracing the dynamic culture of today.

My dear friend, the Musée d'Histoire de Marseille is more than just a museum—it's a time capsule that allows us to travel through the annals of time.

Musée Cantini

My dear friend, let's step into the enchanting world of Musée Cantini—a hidden gem nestled in the heart of Marseille, where art becomes a window into the boundless realms of human creativity. Prepare to be captivated by the eclectic collection of modern and contemporary art that awaits us within these walls.

As we approach Musée Cantini, the historic facade of this former private mansion welcomes us with an air of elegance and sophistication. Once inside, we find ourselves surrounded by a curated selection of artistic masterpieces, each one a testament to the power of expression and the beauty of the human spirit.

The museum's collection showcases an array of artistic movements, from Cubism to Surrealism and everything in between. As we wander through the exhibits, we encounter works by iconic artists who have left an indelible mark on the world of art. Picasso, Braque, Léger, and many other renowned names grace the walls, their creations inviting us to delve into the depths of their imagination.

What makes Musée Cantini truly special is its commitment to celebrating the creativity of regional artists. Local talents are given a platform to shine, and we discover a wealth of contemporary artworks that provide a fresh perspective on the world.

As we move from one room to another, we find ourselves immersed in an ever-changing landscape of colors, shapes, and emotions. Each brushstroke and every artistic gesture seems to tell a story—a glimpse into the artist's soul and a reflection of the world as they see it.

The museum's rotating exhibitions breathe new life into its galleries, ensuring that every visit is a unique experience. From thought-provoking installations to captivating photography, we are exposed to a diverse range of artistic expressions that challenge our perceptions and ignite our curiosity.

Amidst the artistic wonder, the Musée Cantini also serves as a space for contemplation. Secluded corners and cozy nooks allow us to pause, take a deep breath, and absorb the beauty that surrounds us. The museum becomes a sanctuary—a place where art and introspection intertwine.

My dear friend, Musée Cantini is not just a museum—it's a celebration of the boundless creativity of the human spirit. As we bid adieu to this artistic haven, may the memories of the masterpieces we've encountered forever inspire us to seek beauty and expression in every corner of the world.

Musée des Docks Romains (Museum of Roman Docks)

My dear friend, let's embark on a fascinating journey back in time as we step into the Musée des Docks Romains—the Museum of Roman Docks—where the echoes of ancient commerce and maritime splendor come alive before our very eyes. This hidden gem, tucked away beneath the bustling streets of Marseille, holds a treasure trove of archaeological wonders that unveil the city's historic maritime past.

As we descend into the museum's subterranean chambers, a sense of anticipation washes over us. Here, we find ourselves walking through a portal to the Roman era, where Marseille, then known as Massalia, thrived as a bustling port city along the Mediterranean coast.

The museum reveals a remarkably preserved archaeological site—the ancient Roman warehouses and docks that once stood witness to a bustling maritime trade hub. As we stroll through these historic remains, we can almost hear the bustling activity of merchants and sailors, witnesses to the ebb and flow of goods from far-flung corners of the Roman Empire.

The ancient artifacts on display provide a glimpse into the daily lives of those who lived and worked in this bustling port. Amphorae that once carried olive oil, wine, and other precious cargo now stand as silent witnesses to the maritime heritage of Marseille. Stone anchors and maritime equipment remind us of the critical role the sea played in shaping the city's identity.

The museum's interactive exhibits transport us back to the days of ancient commerce. We can visualize the bustling quays, where ships from across the Roman Empire docked to exchange goods, cultures, and ideas. It's as if we are transported to a time when Marseille was a gateway to the world.

As we explore the museum, we gain a deeper understanding of the historical significance of the Roman docks. Marseille's strategic location made it a vital center for maritime trade, connecting the Roman Empire to the riches of the Mediterranean and beyond.

The Musée des Docks Romains stands as a testament to Marseille's enduring spirit—a city that has thrived and reinvented itself across the centuries. It is a reminder of the transformative power of history, as ancient ruins emerge from the depths to inspire and educate future generations.

Mémorial de la Marseillaise (Marseille's Marseillaise Memorial)

My dear friend, let me take you on a poignant journey to the Mémorial de la Marseillaise—the Memorial of Marseille's Marseillaise—an extraordinary place that pays tribute to the iconic French national anthem and the indomitable spirit of Marseille during times of revolution and resistance.

As we approach the memorial, a solemn aura envelops us, and we feel a sense of reverence for the historical significance that this place holds. The Mémorial de la Marseillaise stands as a symbol of hope and resilience, a reminder of the power of music and unity during turbulent times.

The memorial's architecture is a testament to its purpose. The modern facade complements the surrounding historical buildings, seamlessly blending the past and present. As we step inside, we find ourselves immersed in an immersive multimedia experience that brings the story of "La Marseillaise" to life.

The anthem "La Marseillaise" has a storied history, and the museum's exhibits provide context for its origins. We learn how this powerful song became an anthem of the French Revolution, a rallying cry for liberty, and a symbol of resistance against oppression.

As we explore the museum, we encounter interactive displays that allow us to hear the haunting melody and powerful lyrics of "La Marseillaise." The song's impassioned words, penned by Claude Joseph Rouget de Lisle, resonate with revolutionary fervor, capturing the spirit of those who fought for freedom and justice.

The Mémorial de la Marseillaise does not merely recount the anthem's history; it also highlights its significance in shaping the identity of Marseille. We discover how the people of this vibrant city embraced "La Marseillaise" as their own, cherishing its message of hope and unity.

The memorial's displays showcase the song's lasting impact on French history and its enduring legacy as a symbol of national pride. "La Marseillaise" became a unifying force during times of upheaval, reminding us of the strength that music and art can hold in uniting people towards a common purpose.

The museum also delves into the broader themes of liberty and revolution, highlighting the struggles and sacrifices made by those who fought for a better future. It is a powerful reminder of the resilience and determination of the human spirit in the face of adversity.

As we step outside the memorial, we are left with a profound sense of connection to the anthem and the city of Marseille. The Mémorial de la Marseillaise serves as a testament to the enduring power of music, art, and unity in shaping history and defining the essence of a place.

My dear friend, as we bid adieu to the Mémorial de la Marseillaise, may the spirit of "La Marseillaise" forever echo in our hearts. May it remind us of the strength that lies within each of us to stand up for what we believe in and to embrace the unifying power of music and art. And may we carry the story of this iconic anthem with us as a testament to the enduring spirit of Marseille and the unyielding quest for liberty and justice that unites us all.

FRAC Provence-Alpes-Côte d'Azur

My dear friend, let's embark on a journey into the world of contemporary art at FRAC Provence-Alpes-Côte d'Azur—a haven of artistic exploration and innovation that lies at the heart of Marseille. Prepare to be enthralled by the diverse and thought-provoking works of regional artists that grace these walls, inspiring us to see the world from fresh perspectives.

As we approach FRAC, its modern and striking architecture catches our eye—a testament to the institution's commitment to pushing boundaries and embracing the contemporary spirit. The building seems to invite us to step inside and immerse ourselves in the ever-evolving world of art.

Once inside, we find ourselves surrounded by an ever-changing landscape of artistic expression. The museum's rotating exhibitions ensure that every visit is a unique experience, a chance to encounter a new artistic vision and to explore themes that challenge our perceptions and ignite our curiosity.

FRAC Provence-Alpes-Côte d'Azur is dedicated to showcasing the creativity of regional artists. As we move through the galleries, we discover works that speak to the essence of the Provence-Alpes-Côte d'Azur region—the landscapes that have inspired generations of artists, the cultural tapestry that weaves stories of diversity, and the social issues that resonate within the community.

From contemporary paintings and sculptures to multimedia installations and performance art, the museum's collection reflects the boundless diversity of artistic expression. Each artist's unique voice invites us to explore their perspectives and emotions, sparking conversations and connections that transcend boundaries.

The museum also serves as a space for artistic experimentation and education. Interactive displays and workshops offer visitors a chance to engage with art in new ways, encouraging us to become active participants in the creative process.

FRAC's dedication to contemporary art reflects Marseille's dynamic and innovative spirit. As we explore the exhibitions, we feel a sense of inspiration, knowing that we are witnessing the forefront of artistic evolution.

Beyond the visual splendor, FRAC Provence-Alpes-Côte d'Azur becomes a sanctuary for contemplation and reflection. The museum's serene corners and open spaces allow us to pause, take a deep breath, and let the art's emotional resonance wash over us.

Maison Diamantée

My dear friend, allow me to introduce you to the charming Maison Diamantée—an architectural gem tucked away amidst the winding streets of Marseille's historic Panier district. With its unique history and distinctive diamond-shaped facade, this hidden treasure promises to transport us back in time to a bygone era.

As we approach Maison Diamantée, we are immediately captivated by its striking facade—a sight to behold. The diamond-shaped pattern that adorns the building's exterior is a delightful architectural flourish that sets it apart from its neighbors. It's as if the building itself is a precious gem, waiting to reveal its secrets to those who venture within.

Stepping inside, we find ourselves in a cozy and welcoming space where history seems to whisper from every nook and cranny. Maison Diamantée dates back to the 16th century, and its walls bear witness to the passage of time and the stories of those who have inhabited it throughout the centuries.

The interior is a delightful blend of historical charm and modern comforts. The architecture reflects the cultural tapestry of Marseille's past, with influences from various periods—a reminder of the city's rich heritage as a melting pot of cultures.

As we wander through the rooms, we discover that Maison Diamantée has served many roles over the years—a private residence, a workshop, and even an inn for travelers passing through the Panier district. The walls seem to echo with the laughter of families, the chatter of artisans, and the stories of weary travelers finding solace under its roof.

Today, Maison Diamantée houses a small museum that showcases the history of the Panier district and its transformation over time.

Through photographs, artifacts, and interactive exhibits, we gain a deeper understanding of the district's evolution—from a bustling medieval village to a vibrant hub of creativity and culture.

The courtyard of Maison Diamantée beckons us to linger and savor the ambiance. Here, we find ourselves surrounded by the quiet charm of the Panier district—a neighborhood filled with narrow alleyways, quaint shops, and colorful facades. It's a place that invites us to slow down and savor the simple pleasures of life.

As we bid adieu to Maison Diamantée, may the memories of its historical charm and warm embrace stay with us. Let the spirit of this hidden gem inspire us to appreciate the historical treasures that lie within the heart of every city.

Centre de la Vieille Charité (Centre of the Vieille Charité)

My dear friend, let me lead you through the captivating halls of the Centre de la Vieille Charité—a cultural oasis nestled within the historic Vieille Charité complex in Marseille. Prepare to be enchanted by the seamless fusion of history and art as this hidden haven transports us on a journey through time and creativity.

As we approach the Centre de la Vieille Charité, its Baroque architecture stands tall and proud, a testament to the city's rich heritage. Originally built in the 17th century as an almshouse, this historic monument has been lovingly repurposed to house a cultural center that celebrates art, archaeology, and the human spirit.

Stepping through the grand entrance, we are greeted by a serene courtyard—a sanctuary of tranquility amidst the vibrant city life. The soft sound of fountains and the scent of blooming flowers create an atmosphere of peaceful contemplation, inviting us to pause and soak in the ambiance.

As we venture inside, we find ourselves surrounded by a diverse collection of museums and exhibition spaces, each offering a unique glimpse into the artistic and cultural tapestry of Marseille.

The Museum of Mediterranean Archaeology takes us on a journey through the ancient civilizations that once thrived along the Mediterranean coast. The artifacts and relics on display are windows to the past, revealing the lives and traditions of the people who once walked these shores.

The Museum of African, Oceanic, and Native American Arts transports us to far-off lands, celebrating the rich cultural heritage of these diverse regions. The exhibits showcase the artistry and craftsmanship of indigenous peoples, honoring their traditions and stories.

Throughout the center, contemporary art exhibitions add a modern twist to the historic setting. The juxtaposition of ancient walls with cutting-edge installations creates a dialogue between the past and the present, illustrating how art transcends time and connects us all.

As we wander through the galleries, we encounter spaces that foster creativity and learning. Workshops and educational programs invite visitors of all ages to engage with art and culture, ensuring that the Centre de la Vieille Charité remains a living hub of inspiration.

The center's commitment to fostering human connections is reflected in the vibrant community it attracts. It serves as a gathering place for artists, scholars, and enthusiasts from all walks of life, uniting them in a shared appreciation for art and culture.

Musée Regards de Provence

Let me guide you through the enchanting Musée Regards de Provence—a hidden gem that celebrates the beauty and cultural richness of the Provence region, where art becomes a captivating window into the soul of this beloved corner of France.

As we approach Musée Regards de Provence, the building itself catches our eye—a stunning architectural blend of old and new, nestled along the picturesque Quai de la Joliette. The museum's modern facade harmoniously complements the surrounding historical structures, setting the tone for the contemporary treasures that await us inside.

Once we step through the museum's doors, we find ourselves immersed in a world of artistic wonders, each one paying homage to the essence of Provence. The exhibits showcase the region's landscapes, traditions, and cultural heritage, offering us a glimpse into the heart of this cherished corner of the world.

The museum's collection is a testament to the enduring allure of Provence, a land that has inspired artists for centuries. Here, we encounter paintings that capture the vibrant colors of lavender fields, the shimmering waters of the Mediterranean, and the timeless charm of Provençal villages.

As we move from one exhibit to another, we are transported through time and space, exploring the rich tapestry of Provençal life. The artists' brushstrokes and the photographer's lens reveal the joys and struggles of the region's people, their customs, and their intimate connection to the land.

The Musée Regards de Provence is not just a repository of art; it is also a celebration of cultural exchange. Here, we find works by both local and international artists who have been captivated by the allure of Provence. This confluence of perspectives enriches our understanding of the region's significance on the global stage.

The museum's terrace offers a breathtaking panorama of Marseille's Old Port—a serene spot to pause and reflect on the beauty of the city and the region it embraces. It's as if the essence of Provence itself has found its way into this urban haven, inviting us to savor the moment.

The Musée Regards de Provence is more than a place; it is a celebration of the enduring spirit of the region and its people. As we bid adieu to this cultural treasure, may the memories of the art we've encountered forever linger in our hearts. Let the colors, textures, and emotions we've experienced inspire us to cherish the beauty and cultural heritage of every corner of the world.

Secret Gardens and Parks

My dear friend, let me share with you the delightful secret gardens and parks of Marseille—a collection of hidden oases that offer a respite from the city's bustling streets, where nature's beauty and tranquility await to enchant you.

Parc Longchamp

My dear friend, allow me to take you on a personal journey to the enchanting Parc Longchamp—a place close to my heart, where nature's allure and artistic splendor intertwine to create a haven of serenity and inspiration.

As we step into Parc Longchamp, a sense of calm envelops us, and the worries of the world seem to fade away. The gentle rustling of leaves and the soft whispers of the fountains create a symphony of tranquility, inviting us to embrace the moment and savor the beauty that surrounds us.

This park holds a special place in my heart, for it has been my refuge—a sanctuary to escape the daily hustle and rediscover my connection with nature. Whether it's a leisurely morning stroll or an afternoon spent reading beneath the shade of a tree, Parc Longchamp has always welcomed me with open arms, offering solace in its ever-changing landscapes.

The grandeur of the central fountain, with its cascading water and intricate sculptures, never fails to mesmerize me. It stands as a symbol of artistic expression and human creativity, reminding me of the timeless beauty that lies within the heart of Marseille.

The vast green lawns are an invitation to lay down a picnic blanket and enjoy a leisurely meal with loved ones—a moment to share laughter, stories, and the joy of being together.

Parc Longchamp's rose garden is a sensory delight, where the air is filled with the sweet fragrance of blooming flowers. As I wander through the rows of vibrant blooms, I am reminded of the fleeting beauty of life and the importance of cherishing every precious moment.

The hidden corners of the park beckon me to explore further, unveiling small ponds teeming with aquatic life and meandering paths that lead to charming surprises—a forgotten sculpture, a quiet bench with a view, or a playful squirrel curiously observing passersby.

In every season, Parc Longchamp reveals a different facet of its charm. From the vibrant colors of spring to the golden hues of autumn, each visit brings a renewed sense of wonder and gratitude for the natural wonders that grace our lives.

But beyond its natural allure, Parc Longchamp holds a deeper significance—the memories woven into its very fabric. It has been a witness to my joys and sorrows, a companion in moments of reflection, and a place where I've found inspiration for my creative pursuits.

Jardin des Vestiges (Garden of Remains)

My dear friend, let me lead you to the intriguing Jardin des Vestiges—the Garden of Remains—a place where history and nature gracefully converge and the ancient echoes of Marseille's past resonate through time.

As we step into the Jardin des Vestiges, the air seems to carry the whispers of bygone eras. This hidden gem, nestled near the Vieux Port, holds the remnants of ancient civilizations that once thrived on this very land. It is a unique haven where nature intertwines with the echoes of the past, creating an atmosphere of both tranquility and intrigue.

The garden's pathways wind their way through archaeological ruins dating back to the Greek and Roman periods, and every step unveils the stories of those who once walked these streets. The stones beneath our feet carry the weight of centuries, reminding us of the timeless nature of history and the lives that have shaped the city we see today.

As we explore the garden, the remains of ancient walls and structures become windows into the past—a glimpse of the architectural prowess of past civilizations and the marks they left on the land. The fragments of columns and statues tell tales of grandeur, while the ancient tombs offer insights into the beliefs and customs of these ancient peoples.

Nature has embraced these ruins, softening their edges with the passage of time. Delicate vines crawl up ancient stones, and wildflowers bloom between the crevices—a living testament to the resilience of life amidst the remnants of history.

The garden's design is a harmonious blend of history and contemporary artistry. Thoughtful lighting and subtle landscaping create an ambiance of reverence, as if inviting us to reflect on the significance of the past and its connection to the present.

Jardin des Vestiges serves as a bridge between generations—a place where modern-day visitors can connect with the ancient souls that once walked these streets. It is a reminder that beneath the surface of our bustling city lie the stories of those who have come before us, shaping Marseille's identity and culture.

As we bid adieu to the Jardin des Vestiges, may its echoes linger in our hearts. Let the beauty of this garden of remains inspire us to appreciate the historical treasures that lie hidden within the heart of every city. And may we carry the essence of this special place with us as a reminder of the significance of our shared history and the lasting connections we hold with those who walked these streets long before us.

Parc Borély

My dear friend, let me take you on a delightful journey to Parc Borély—a serene oasis of natural beauty and tranquility nestled along the coast of Marseille. With its lush landscapes, serene lakes, and fragrant gardens, this hidden gem offers a sanctuary where one can embrace the essence of nature and find solace amidst the city's vibrant energy.

As we enter Parc Borély, the gentle rustling of leaves and the chirping of birds welcome us with a soothing melody. The park's vast green lawns stretch out like a soft carpet, inviting us to kick off our shoes and bask in the simple joy of feeling the earth beneath our feet.

In the heart of the park, we discover a serene lake, its surface mirroring the clear blue sky above. As we walk along its shores, we find ourselves captivated by the graceful swans gliding across the water—a scene straight out of a fairytale.

The fragrant rose gardens of Parc Borély offer an intoxicating sensory experience. The vibrant colors and sweet scents of blooming roses enchant our senses, as if inviting us to stop and savor the beauty that surrounds us.

As we explore further, we encounter a hidden treasure—the Jardin des Plantes. This botanical garden is a celebration of biodiversity, with a diverse array of plant species from around the world. Here, we can embark on a botanical journey, discovering the intricate details of each plant's life and the fascinating stories they hold.

The park's design encourages leisure and relaxation. We find secluded benches and shaded alcoves, perfect for a moment of quiet contemplation or an afternoon spent lost in the pages of a favorite book.

Beyond the natural beauty, Parc Borély offers recreational activities for all. From picnics on the grass to paddle boating on the lake, the park becomes a playground for both the young and the young at heart.

Parc Borély is more than just a park—it is a sanctuary for the soul, a place where one can escape the hustle of everyday life and reconnect with the simplicity and serenity of nature.

My dear friend, as we bid adieu to Parc Borély, may its enchanting beauty stay with us forever.

Let the memories of this tranquil haven remind us of the importance of finding moments of peace amidst life's busyness. And may we continue to seek out these intimate escapes, where nature's embrace rejuvenates our spirit and allows us to appreciate the timeless wonders that surround us in every corner of the world.

Jardin de la Colline Puget (Puget Hill Garden)

My dear friend, let me lead you to the picturesque Jardin de la Colline Puget—the Puget Hill Garden—an enchanting sanctuary nestled atop a hillside, offering breathtaking views of Marseille's Old Port and a captivating blend of nature and art.

As we ascend to the Jardin de la Colline Puget, the anticipation of discovering its hidden treasures fills the air. The climb rewards us with sweeping vistas of Marseille's bustling harbor and the azure waters of the Mediterranean—a mesmerizing sight that instantly captivates the soul.

The garden's design exudes an air of tranquility, inviting us to wander along meandering paths lined with lush vegetation and vibrant blooms. The carefully curated landscaping enhances the natural beauty of the hillside, creating a serene escape where we can immerse ourselves in the embrace of nature.

As we explore further, we encounter elegant sculptures scattered throughout the garden, each one a testament to the artistic vision of the Puget brothers—the talented artists who once lived on this very hill. These sculptures add a touch of elegance and grace to the already enchanting setting, their forms seeming to come alive against the backdrop of the cityscape.

As we stroll along the terraced garden, we find quiet corners with stone benches that beckon us to sit and marvel at the captivating views below. It's as if time slows down, allowing us to savor the simple pleasure of being present in the moment and to admire the symphony of colors and scents that fill the air.

The Jardin de la Colline Puget is a haven for creativity and inspiration. The idyllic setting, with its panoramic views, has inspired countless artists, writers, and dreamers throughout the years. It's a place where we can feel our own creativity awaken and our thoughts flow freely as we allow the beauty of our surroundings to ignite our imagination.

Parc du 26ème Centenaire

My dear friend, let me introduce you to the delightful Parc du 26ème Centenaire—a hidden gem tucked away in the heart of Marseille, where nature's beauty and artistic elements blend harmoniously to create a serene and enchanting oasis.

As we step into Parc du 26ème Centenaire, the soft whispers of the breeze and the gentle rustling of leaves welcome us into this peaceful sanctuary. The park's name commemorates the 2600th anniversary of the foundation of the city of Marseille, and it is a place where history and modernity intertwine to offer a unique and memorable experience.

The park's design is a delightful fusion of traditional French gardens and contemporary elements, creating a harmonious symphony of visual beauty. Lush green lawns stretch out like a verdant carpet, inviting us to lay down a picnic blanket and bask in the warm embrace of the sun.

Colorful flowerbeds dot the landscape, each one a vibrant tapestry of blooms that adds a splash of charm to the park's tranquil setting. As we meander through the pathways, the scents of lavender, roses, and other fragrant flowers enchant our senses, creating an intimate connection with nature.

The park's centerpiece is a magnificent sculpture—a grand contemporary fountain—that seems to dance with water in graceful movements. Its elegant design is a captivating sight, drawing us closer to admire the artistry and craftsmanship that went into creating this masterpiece.

Parc du 26ème Centenaire offers more than just natural beauty. It is a place for communal gatherings and cultural events where locals and visitors alike come together to celebrate art and creativity. Concerts, art exhibitions, and other cultural happenings infuse the park with a vibrant energy, transforming it into a lively hub of artistic expression.

As we explore the park's hidden corners, we discover peaceful alcoves adorned with sculptures and artwork, offering moments of introspection and contemplation. These artistic touches remind us of the enduring connection between nature and human creativity—a reminder that art and nature can coexist in perfect harmony.

Jardin du Pharo (Pharo Garden)

My dear friend, allow me to whisk you away to the breathtaking Jardin du Pharo—the Pharo Garden—a place of beauty, history, and captivating views that grace the city of Marseille. Perched atop a hill near the iconic Palais du Pharo, this hidden oasis offers a tapestry of natural wonders and a sense of tranquility that envelops the soul.

As we step into the Jardin du Pharo, the azure expanse of the Mediterranean Sea stretches out before us, shimmering like a precious gem under the warm Mediterranean sun. The garden's vantage point provides panoramic views of the Old Port, the sparkling waters, and the city's charming architecture, instantly inviting us to embark on a journey of discovery.

The gentle scent of the sea breeze mingles with the fragrance of blooming flowers, creating an intoxicating symphony of scents that elevates the senses. The garden's well-tended flowerbeds burst with colors, their vibrant petals swaying in harmony with the coastal winds—a true testament to nature's artistry.

Secluded alcoves and shady pathways lead us through the garden, revealing hidden corners perfect for contemplation. Here, we find peaceful moments to savor the beauty that surrounds us and to reflect on the timeless allure of Marseille and its connection to the vast expanse of the sea.

The garden's allure is heightened by the presence of the Palais du Pharo, a majestic palace built by Napoleon III for Empress Eugénie. The palace's elegant architecture adds a touch of grandeur to the garden, a reminder of the city's rich history and its significance as a beacon of culture and beauty.

As we stroll further, we come across picturesque terraces that seem to reach out towards the sea, inviting us to linger and lose ourselves in the ever-changing hues of the horizon. The gentle lapping of waves against the rocks below and the distant hum of city life create a captivating symphony of sounds that harmonize with the tranquil atmosphere.

Jardin du Pharo not only delights the senses but also serves as a beloved gathering spot for locals and visitors alike. Families, friends, and couples gather to bask in the park's splendor, creating an ambiance of conviviality and shared appreciation for the natural wonders that surround them.

Jardin de la Magalone (Magalone Garden)

My dear friend, come with me to discover the enchanting Jardin de la Magalone—the Magalone Garden—a hidden paradise that lies tucked away in the 9th arrondissement of Marseille. As we step into this idyllic sanctuary, a sense of serenity envelops us, and we are transported to a world of natural beauty and timeless charm.

The Jardin de la Magalone is a true hidden gem, known only to those who have sought out its tranquil embrace. As we enter, we are greeted by the gentle rustling of leaves and the soft chirping of birds, creating a symphony of nature's melodies that soothe the soul.

This lush garden is a masterpiece of design and landscaping, with carefully manicured lawns, meandering pathways, and delightful flowerbeds that bloom in an array of colors. The fragrance of blooming flowers fills the air, creating an intoxicating atmosphere that beckons us to explore further.

As we wander deeper into the garden, we discover hidden corners adorned with charming statues and ornate fountains, adding a touch of elegance and artistry to the natural beauty that surrounds us. Each sculpture seems to have a story to tell, as if they are guardians of the garden's secrets, whispering tales of the past to those who care to listen.

The garden's design embraces a sense of harmony with nature, as if the landscape itself is a work of art, carefully curated to bring joy and serenity to those who seek respite within its bounds. It's a place where one can find solace in the simple beauty of nature, away from the hustle and bustle of the city.

The Jardin de la Magalone offers many secluded alcoves and benches, inviting us to sit and revel in the moment. Here, we can lose ourselves in a good book, enjoy a leisurely chat with a loved one, or simply take a moment for quiet reflection amidst the beauty that surrounds us.

This hidden oasis is also a favorite spot for locals seeking a peaceful escape. Families, friends, and couples come here to enjoy picnics on the grass, surrounded by nature's embrace—a cherished opportunity to connect with loved ones and create lasting memories.

Unique Local Experiences

My dear friend, let me take you on a journey to discover the unique local experiences that await you in Marseille—a city teeming with vibrant culture, history, and a spirit of adventure. From savoring the flavors of the local cuisine to immersing yourself in the warmth of the community, Marseille offers a treasure trove of unforgettable moments.

Fish Market at Vieux Port

My dear friend, let me take you on a sensory journey to the bustling Fish Market at Vieux Port—a place where the heartbeat of Marseille meets the rhythm of the sea. Here, time seems to slow down as we immerse ourselves in the vibrant colors, lively sounds, and delectable aromas that fill the air.

As we approach the Vieux Port in the early hours of the morning, the first rays of sunlight kiss the rippling waters, creating a mesmerizing dance of light and shadow. The air is infused with the salty tang of the sea, a gentle reminder that we are about to witness a time-honored tradition—the spectacle of fishing boats returning from their nocturnal journeys.

As we draw nearer, the vibrant atmosphere of the Fish Market comes alive. The sound of seagulls overhead and the gentle clinking of boats against the harbor echo through the air, mingling with the animated chatter of fishermen and locals alike.

Rows of wooden stands are adorned with an impressive display of the day's catch—glistening fish of all shapes and sizes, prawns, scallops, and a rainbow of sea treasures that beckon us to explore further. The fishermen, with weathered faces and hands hardened by the sea, proudly display their offerings with a deep sense of pride and love for their craft.

Engaging with the local vendors, we discover a warmth and friendliness that are uniquely Marseille. They share stories of the sea, tales of their ancestors who braved the waves before them, and the importance of preserving the city's maritime heritage.

As the market buzzes with life, we can't help but be drawn to the culinary delights awaiting us. Our senses are delighted as we savor the aroma of freshly grilled fish, mingling with the scent of herbs and spices used in traditional recipes passed down through generations.

Sampling the local cuisine is a true feast for the senses. From the iconic bouillabaisse—a rich and hearty fish stew—to delicate seafood platters, every dish tells a story of Marseille's coastal bounty.

At the Fish Market, we not only experience the culinary riches but also witness the essence of Marseille's maritime soul. It's a place where the heartbeat of the city converges with the rhythm of the sea—a reminder of the deep connection between the people of Marseille and the bountiful waters that have sustained them for centuries.

Calanques Boat Tour

My dear friend, let me take you on a thrilling Calanques Boat Tour—an adventure that will immerse you in the awe-inspiring beauty of Marseille's Calanques National Park. Brace yourself for an unforgettable journey as we set sail to explore the hidden treasures of the Mediterranean coastline.

As we board the boat, a sense of excitement fills the air. The turquoise waters glisten in the sunlight, and the rugged limestone cliffs rise majestically, beckoning us to venture deeper into their enchanting embrace.

Our boat glides effortlessly over the gentle waves, revealing breathtaking views of the coastline. The sea breeze caresses our skin, and the salty aroma of the sea invigorates our senses, reminding us that we are embarking on an authentic maritime experience.

The captain, a seasoned local with a passion for the sea, regales us with fascinating stories about the history, geology, and biodiversity of the Calanques. We learn about the ancient geological forces that sculpted these magnificent cliffs over millennia and the incredible diversity of plant and marine life that call this rugged landscape home.

As we venture further into the heart of the Calanques, we encounter hidden coves with crystal-clear waters, inviting us to take a refreshing dip in the Mediterranean's embrace. The sea reveals its secrets as we catch glimpses of colorful fish darting beneath the boat and perhaps even catch sight of a playful dolphin or two dancing in the waves.

The Calanques' limestone walls rise dramatically around us, creating a sense of intimacy and wonder. Time seems to stand still as we navigate through narrow channels, marveling at the geological wonders that nature has bestowed upon this coastal paradise.

Our boat glides to a serene stop, and we find ourselves surrounded by tranquility. The captain cuts the engine, and we are embraced by a silence interrupted only by the soft sounds of waves lapping against the cliffs—a moment of blissful serenity that stays with us forever.

We savor a delightful onboard picnic, feasting on local delicacies and sipping chilled beverages. As we indulge in the flavors of the region, we feel a deep sense of connection to the land and sea, understanding that this experience is a celebration of Marseille's natural bounty.

As the sun begins its gentle descent towards the horizon, we make our way back to the port. The sky paints a canvas of colors—a breathtaking farewell to a day filled with wonder and adventure.

Pétanque with Locals

My dear friend, let me lead you to a heartwarming and delightful experience—playing Pétanque with the locals in Marseille. This cherished French ball game is not just a sport; it's a cherished tradition that brings people together, fostering camaraderie and a sense of community.

As we arrive at a sunny square or a cozy park, we are greeted by the sight of locals engaged in spirited Pétanque matches. Smiles and laughter fill the air, and the clinking of metal boules adds a musical touch to the ambiance.

Approaching the players with curiosity and excitement, we find the locals to be warm and welcoming, inviting us to join in on the fun. Without hesitation, we become part of the

Pétanque family—a diverse group of individuals from all walks of life, united by their love for this beloved game.

The rules of Pétanque are simple, yet the game demands skill, strategy, and a touch of finesse. The players eagerly share their tips and tricks, making us feel right at home in this friendly atmosphere.

As we take our place on the gravel court, we grasp the steel boules in our hands, feeling the cool weight and texture. The game begins, and our focus is solely on the smooth gravel and the small wooden jack—the target to aim for. The air is filled with friendly banter and encouragement as we take turns throwing the boules, each shot accompanied by cheers or good-natured taunts.

The game transcends the mere act of throwing metal balls; it becomes a dance of strategy, skill, and camaraderie. Every shot taken is an opportunity to connect with the locals, share laughter, and forge new friendships.

Win or lose, the joy of the game lies not in the outcome but in the shared experience. We bask in the warmth of the Marseille community, realizing that Pétanque is more than just a pastime—it's a tradition that unites generations, transcending language and cultural barriers.

After a lively game, we gather with our newfound friends, enjoying refreshments and sharing stories. We feel a sense of belonging, knowing that we are now part of a tapestry of shared memories and connections that stretch far beyond the boundaries of the Pétanque court.

As the sun begins to set, casting a golden glow over the square, we bid farewell to our Pétanque companions. The memory of this heartwarming experience will forever hold a special place in our hearts—a reminder that the true essence of travel lies not just in sightseeing but in connecting with the heart and soul of a place through the people who call it home.

Panier District Walking Tour

My dear friend, come with me on a delightful Panier District Walking Tour—a journey that will lead us through the heart and soul of Marseille's oldest and most charming neighborhood. As we step into the cobbled streets of the Panier, we are transported back in time, surrounded by a captivating blend of history, art, and vibrant culture.

The Panier District is a labyrinth of narrow alleys and hidden squares, each one telling a tale of Marseille's rich past. As we walk along the cobblestones, the colorful facades of traditional Provençal houses rise before us, adorned with flower-filled balconies—a true feast for the eyes.

As we meander through the district, we discover charming artisan workshops where local craftsmen showcase their skills and share the secrets of their trade. The scent of fresh-baked bread wafts through the air, inviting us to taste traditional Provençal treats and artisanal delights that have been passed down through generations.

The Panier is also a haven for artists and creatives. We encounter vibrant street art adorning walls and façades, each mural telling a unique story of Marseille's vibrant contemporary art scene. The neighborhood's bohemian spirit is palpable, inspiring us to embrace our own creativity and appreciation for the beauty that surrounds us.

Hidden squares invite us to pause and take in the tranquil ambiance. Here, locals gather to chat and share laughter, forging bonds that have woven the fabric of Panier's close-knit community. We feel a sense of belonging, as if we, too, have become part of this cherished neighborhood's tapestry.

The Panier is also home to a wealth of boutiques and galleries, each offering a carefully curated selection of artisanal products and local art. Here, we have the opportunity to find unique souvenirs and support Marseille's vibrant creative community.

As the tour draws to a close, we find ourselves in a picturesque square. The gentle murmur of the fountain provides a soothing soundtrack, and the old-fashioned lamp posts cast a warm glow, as if the Panier itself is bidding us farewell.

Marseille Street Art Hunt

My dear friend, let's embark on an exciting Marseille Street Art Hunt—a journey of discovery through the city's vibrant and ever-changing urban art scene. As we set out to explore the streets of Marseille, we open our hearts and minds to the hidden treasures that await us on the walls and alleys.

Our eyes are on the lookout for splashes of color, intricate designs, and thought-provoking murals that adorn the city's facades. Each piece of street art tells a unique story, reflecting the perspectives, emotions, and creativity of the artists who left their mark on the city.

As we wander through the neighborhoods, we find ourselves in a living outdoor gallery where every wall becomes a canvas for artistic expression. The art is diverse and eclectic, ranging from bold graffiti to delicate stencils and from larger-than-life murals to tiny hidden gems that reward those who take the time to seek them out.

But street art is ever-changing, and so is Marseille's urban canvas. We soon discover that the hunt is not just about finding the art but also about being present in the moment and embracing the unexpected surprises that await us around every corner.

As we delve deeper into the labyrinthine streets, we engage with the local community and fellow art enthusiasts who share our passion for the creative spirit of Marseille. Conversations flow easily, and we bond over our shared appreciation for the artists' talents and the stories they tell.

As the sun begins to set, casting a golden glow on the city's walls, we feel a sense of fulfillment and wonder. Our Street Art Hunt has been more than just an adventure; it has been a celebration of self-expression, creativity, and the vibrant energy that pulses through the city's veins.

Marseille Soap Workshop

My dear friend, let's embark on a delightful Marseille Soap Workshop—a hands-on experience that will take us on a journey into the traditional art of soap-making, a cherished craft that has been perfected in Marseille for centuries.

As we step into the workshop, the air is filled with the soothing scents of natural ingredients—olive oil, lavender, and other fragrant essences—that will soon become the building blocks of our handmade soaps. The workshop is a haven of creativity, with colorful molds, artisanal packaging, and an array of natural ingredients waiting to be transformed into exquisite bars of soap.

The first step is to carefully measure and mix the ingredients. We learn that authentic Marseille soap is made with a simple recipe—pure olive oil, alkaline ash, and sea salt—ingredients that have remained unchanged for centuries, resulting in a soap that is gentle on the skin and environmentally friendly.

With our hands immersed in the silky-smooth mixture, we feel a sense of connection to the ancient traditions that have shaped Marseille's soap-making heritage. The guide shares stories of the city's soap-making history, dating back to the 6th century, when soap was first crafted in large cauldrons along the Mediterranean coast.

Next, we pour the soap mixture into beautifully crafted molds, adding a touch of creativity by incorporating natural colors and fragrances. The anticipation of seeing our creations take shape fills us with excitement, and we wait eagerly for the soap to set.

As the soap hardens, we explore the workshop further, discovering shelves adorned with an assortment of artisanal soaps made by skilled local soapmakers. Each bar tells its own story—some infused with lavender for relaxation, others with rosemary for rejuvenation—creating a tapestry of scents and textures that reflect the diversity of the region.

Finally, our soaps are ready, and we carefully remove them from the molds. The feeling of accomplishment and pride washes over us as we held our handmade creations in our hands. The soaps are a testament to our creativity and a connection to the heritage of Marseille's time-honored craft.

Leaving the workshop with our handcrafted soaps in hand, we carry a piece of Marseille's essence with us—an artisanal souvenir that reflects the city's dedication to craftsmanship and the beauty of simplicity.

Corsican Food Experience

My dear friend, let's embark on a tantalizing Corsican Food Experience—a journey that will take us on a culinary adventure through the flavors of this beautiful Mediterranean island, right here in the heart of Marseille.

Corsican cuisine is a delightful fusion of French and Italian influences, boasting a rich tapestry of flavors and ingredients that reflect the island's unique geography and cultural heritage.

As we step into the restaurant, we are greeted with a warm smile and a rustic ambiance that evokes the spirit of Corsica. The decor transports us to the sun-kissed shores, adorned with seashells, fishing nets, and images of the island's breathtaking landscapes.

Our journey begins with the quintessential Corsican charcuterie—a tantalizing platter of cured meats that includes coppa, lonzu, and figatellu, all sourced from local farms. Each bite is a symphony of flavors, an ode to the island's deep-rooted tradition of preserving meats using time-honored techniques.

Next, we delve into the world of Corsican cheeses—delicate brocciu, tangy fromage de brebis, and the famous tomme corse. Paired with fragrant honey from the island's maquis shrubland, the cheeses delight our taste buds and offer a glimpse into the island's pastoral heritage.

Our journey continues with hearty stews and savory pies—Corsican classics that pay homage to the bountiful land and sea. We savor the flavors of wild boar stew, tender lamb simmered with aromatic herbs, and delicate fish bouillabaisse, each dish capturing the essence of Corsica's rugged landscape and maritime bounty.

Accompanying our meal is a selection of fine Corsican wines—vermentinu, niellucciu, and sciaccarellu—varieties that flourish in the island's sun-drenched vineyards. The wines complement the dishes, creating a harmonious pairing that celebrates Corsica's unique terroir.

Our feast concludes with a sweet symphony of desserts, featuring the island's signature chestnut flour cake—fiadone—alongside flaky canistrelli biscuits and indulgent fiadone cheesecake. Each dessert is a celebration of Corsican traditions and the island's abundant harvest of chestnuts and aromatic herbs.

Throughout the meal, we are regaled with stories of Corsica's culinary heritage—the centuries-old recipes passed down through generations, the sense of community fostered by sharing meals, and the profound connection between the island's people and the land they call home.

Sunset Picnic at Corniche

My dear friend, let's embark on a magical Sunset Picnic at Corniche—a breathtaking experience that will fill our hearts with wonder and our souls with tranquility as we witness the sun bid adieu to the day, painting the skies in hues of gold and crimson.

As we make our way to the Corniche, the anticipation of the evening's spectacle fills the air. The road clings to the coastline, offering panoramic views of the Mediterranean Sea that stretch as far as the eye can see. The sea breeze gently caresses our skin, and the rhythmic sound of crashing waves creates a serene soundtrack to our journey.

Upon arrival, we find the perfect spot—a quiet and secluded corner overlooking the azure waters. The panoramic view of Marseille's coastline unfolds before us like a living painting, a tapestry of nature's beauty that takes our breath away.

We lay out our picnic blanket and unpack the delicacies we've brought to savor. The selection is a true celebration of Mediterranean flavors—freshly baked baguettes, artisanal cheeses, olives, juicy cherry tomatoes, and plump grapes that burst with sweetness.

A bottle of fine local wine awaits, eager to be uncorked, as we prepare to toast to the marvels of nature and the joy of being present in this precious moment. The first sip takes us on a journey through the sun-soaked vineyards of Provence, where the terroir is reflected in every drop.

As the sun begins its slow descent towards the horizon, we find ourselves captivated by the changing colors of the sky. The golden glow bathes the coastline, casting a warm embrace on the city's iconic landmarks—the Vieux Port, Basilique Notre-Dame de la Garde, and the silhouettes of boats sailing into the dusk.

Time seems to stand still as we revel in the beauty of the sunset, sharing stories, laughter, and quiet moments of reflection. The world around us fades away, leaving only the gentle sound of the waves and the company of a dear friend to cherish.

As the last rays of the sun dip below the horizon, the sky transforms into a canvas of pastel hues, a symphony of pinks, oranges, and purples that mirrors the beauty of our surroundings. We sit in awe, grateful for the opportunity to witness such natural wonder.

And as the stars begin to twinkle in the darkening sky, we know that this Sunset Picnic at Corniche will forever remain etched in our hearts. Let the memory of this enchanting evening remind us to embrace the simple joys of life—to savor the beauty of nature, the warmth of friendship, and the peace that comes with being present in the moment.

Chapter 5: Marseille's Neighborhoods

Le Panier: Marseille's Historic Quarter

Dear fellow traveler, let me take you on a journey through the enchanting streets of Le Panier—a time-honored district that weaves the tapestry of Marseille's history and soul. As we step into this charming neighborhood, we step back in time, immersing ourselves in a world of narrow alleys, quaint squares, and stories that have shaped the heart of Marseille.

Le Panier, Marseille's oldest quarter, is a place of contrasts and character. The ancient Greek settlers founded the city on these very streets over 2,600 years ago, and its rich heritage is evident at every turn.

As we wander through the cobblestone streets, the scent of freshly baked bread and coffee fills the air, inviting us to explore further. The facades of pastel-colored buildings bear the marks of time, each crack and weathered paint telling a story of resilience and history.

The locals we encounter are warm and friendly, with hearts as vibrant as the colorful shutters that adorn their homes. Their laughter and animated conversations echo through the alleys, making us feel like we've become part of a close-knit community that cherishes its traditions.

At the heart of Le Panier lies the Vieille Charité, a historical gem that exudes a sense of elegance and grace. This former hospice, with its majestic arcades and ornate façade, now houses museums and cultural institutions, reflecting Marseille's commitment to preserving its heritage while embracing the spirit of creativity.

As we explore further, we stumble upon hidden squares—oases of tranquility adorned with bubbling fountains and shady trees. Locals gather here to chat, play Pétanque, and bask in the simple joys of life. We, too, take a moment to pause and absorb the beauty of the moment, feeling a profound connection to the soul of Le Panier.

Artistic expression is abundant in this vibrant quarter. Street art adorns walls and facades, providing a canvas for contemporary artists to share their messages and talents. The juxtaposition of ancient architecture and modern art adds to the district's allure, bridging the gap between the past and the present.

Le Panier is also a haven for artisans and creatives. Art galleries, craft workshops, and boutique stores line the streets, offering unique treasures waiting to be discovered. We find ourselves captivated by the handcrafted goods that showcase the talent and passion of local artisans.

As we bid adieu to Le Panier, we carry with us the essence of this historic quarter—a place that captures the essence of Marseille's past and present. Let the stories of its ancient streets and the vibrancy of its community inspire us to cherish the heritage of every place we visit, embracing the intimate and authentic experiences that make our travels unforgettable.

La Plaine: Bohemian Vibe and Street Markets

Let me whisk you away to the vibrant and bohemian neighborhood of La Plaine—a place that exudes an artistic and eclectic spirit, where the soul of Marseille comes alive in the hustle and bustle of lively street markets.

As we step into La Plaine, we are greeted by a kaleidoscope of colors and sounds. The air is infused with the aroma of freshly brewed coffee, and the music of street musicians fills the streets, creating an ambiance that celebrates the free-spirited nature of this unique quarter.

La Plaine is a melting pot of cultures and creativity—a haven for artists, musicians, and bohemian souls. The facades of buildings are adorned with vibrant street art, reflecting the neighborhood's love for artistic expression and its embrace of diversity.

Our journey begins at the bustling Cours Julien, a square that serves as the heart of La Plaine. Here, locals and visitors alike gather to soak in the bohemian vibe, chat with friends at lively cafes, and peruse the colorful boutiques that line the streets.

As we explore further, we stumble upon street markets that offer a treasure trove of delights. The Marché de la Plaine is a true feast for the senses, with stalls brimming with fresh fruits, vegetables, and aromatic herbs—ingredients that form the backbone of Mediterranean cuisine.

Local artisans proudly display their handcrafted goods, from intricate jewelry to quirky art pieces. The market is a celebration of creativity, where every creation carries the essence of the artist's spirit.

La Plaine is also known for its lively flea markets, where vintage treasures and second-hand goods find new life in the hands of appreciative collectors. We delight in the thrill of the hunt, uncovering unique finds and hidden gems that hold a piece of Marseille's history.

At the heart of La Plaine lies a sense of community—a place where neighbors know each other by name and newcomers are welcomed with open arms. The friendly exchanges and laughter that fill the streets create a sense of belonging, making us feel like we are part of this bohemian family.

As the sun begins to set, casting a warm glow over La Plaine, we find ourselves drawn to a local gathering spot. Here, musicians play impromptu concerts, and locals gather to dance and celebrate the simple joys of life. We join in the festivities, feeling the rhythms of Marseille pulsating through our veins.

As we bid adieu to La Plaine, we carry with us the spirit of this bohemian neighborhood—a place that celebrates creativity, embraces diversity, and cherishes the beauty of the everyday. Let the essence of La Plaine inspire us to live with open hearts, to celebrate art and community, and to cherish the moments we share with kindred spirits on our journey through life.

Cours Julien: Artsy and Lively District

Let's venture into the artsy and lively district of Cours Julien—a place where creativity knows no bounds and the spirit of Marseille's vibrant art scene comes to life in every colorful corner.

As we step into Cours Julien, we are greeted by a feast of colors and a symphony of artistic expression. The streets are adorned with colorful murals, graffiti, and street art, transforming the district into an open-air gallery that captivates the imagination.

The bohemian spirit is palpable in Cours Julien, attracting artists, musicians, and free-spirited souls who embrace the beauty of individuality and creative freedom. The locals here have an infectious passion for art, and the energy of their artistic endeavors is contagious.

As we stroll through the district, we encounter quirky boutiques, vintage stores, and art galleries that offer a curated selection of handcrafted goods and unique finds. Each shop is a treasure trove of creativity, showcasing the talents of local artisans who infuse their creations with heart and soul.

Cafes and restaurants spill out onto the sidewalks, inviting us to take a seat and indulge in culinary delights while absorbing the vibrant atmosphere around us. The air is filled with the aroma of freshly brewed coffee and the chatter of friends engaged in animated conversations.

The heart of Cours Julien is the central square, a gathering place that serves as a stage for impromptu performances and street artists. Musicians fill the air with melodies, and dancers sway to the rhythm of life, creating an ever-changing tapestry of artistic expression.

The district's bohemian nature extends to the people we encounter—friendly and open, with a zest for life and an appreciation for the arts. Conversations flow easily, and we find ourselves immersed in the shared passion for creativity and the celebration of the human spirit.

Cours Julien is a hub of cultural events and festivals that bring the community together. Art exhibitions, live performances, and poetry readings are regular occurrences, fostering a sense of belonging and inspiring collaboration among artists and enthusiasts.

As the sun begins to set, casting a warm glow over the streets, we feel a sense of gratitude for the experience of being in this artsy and lively district. The creativity that surrounds us ignites a spark within, reminding us of the boundless possibilities of self-expression.

The Old Port (Vieux Port): The Heart of the City

Dear fellow traveler, let us set sail on a journey to the very heart of Marseille—the Old Port, known as Vieux Port—a place where the city's soul and maritime heritage come together in a beautiful dance of history and modern life.

As we approach the Old Port, we are greeted by the sight of gently bobbing boats, their sails unfurled, and the shimmering waters that have witnessed centuries of maritime tales. The air is infused with the salty scent of the sea, carrying with it the whispers of the past and the promises of new adventures.

The Old Port has been the beating heart of Marseille for over 2,600 years, and its significance as a bustling trading hub and a gateway to the world has left an indelible mark on the city's identity. Today, it continues to be a lively and dynamic place—a meeting point for locals and visitors alike, where cultures converge and stories are shared.

As we stroll along the quays, we are drawn to the colorful fish market—a true feast for the senses. The day's catch is displayed with pride, and the vendors' animated calls echo through the air, adding to the vibrant atmosphere. Here, we find the freshest seafood, caught from the very waters that surround us—a true testament to Marseille's close bond with the sea.

The Old Port is also a place of leisure and relaxation. Cafes and restaurants line the waterfront, inviting us to take a seat and savor the flavors of Mediterranean cuisine while gazing out at the boats gliding gracefully by. The clinking of glasses and the laughter of friends fill the air, creating a sense of camaraderie that is as timeless as the sea itself.

At the heart of the port stands the iconic Basilique Notre-Dame de la Garde, perched on a hill overlooking the city. Its golden statue of the Virgin Mary, known as "La Bonne Mère," watches over Marseille, providing solace and protection to sailors and residents alike. The basilica is a symbol of hope and unity—a beacon that guides ships home and welcomes travelers to the heart of the city.

As the sun begins to set, painting the sky in hues of gold and pink, we find ourselves captivated by the beauty of the Old Port. The charm of this historic harbor is eternal, and the stories it holds are a testament to the resilience and spirit of Marseille and its people.

La Corniche: Stunning Sea Views

Oh, my dear friend, let's embark on a journey along La Corniche—a breathtaking coastal road that unveils some of the most stunning sea views in all of Marseille. As we wind along this scenic route, we are treated to a mesmerizing display of the Mediterranean's azure waters meeting the rugged coastline in a dance of harmony and beauty.

La Corniche is a true feast for the eyes, where the sea and the sky seem to merge in a poetic embrace. The road hugs the cliffside, revealing hidden coves and secluded beaches below—a haven for sunbathers and swimmers seeking solace by the sea.

With every turn, new panoramas unfold before us—images that artists and poets alike have sought to capture in their works. The sunlight dances on the water, creating a dazzling play of reflections that enraptures our senses and fills us with wonder.

The coastal breeze gently caresses our skin, carrying the scent of salt and the warmth of the Mediterranean sun. We feel a profound connection to the sea and the natural world, a reminder of the beauty and vastness of the universe we are privileged to witness.

Along La Corniche, we encounter charming cafés and restaurants with outdoor terraces, each one offering the perfect setting to enjoy a leisurely meal with a backdrop of sea and sky. The aroma of freshly grilled seafood and the clinking of glasses create a sense of indulgence and relaxation.

The coastal road also leads us to some of Marseille's most beloved landmarks—the iconic Vallon des Auffes, a picturesque fishing village nestled in a tiny harbor, and the majestic Château d'If, perched on a rocky island in the distance—a symbol of maritime history and intrigue.

As we pause to take in the beauty around us, we find that time seems to stand still along La Corniche. The sea views beckon us to immerse ourselves in the present moment, to savor the simple pleasures of life, and to revel in the grandeur of nature's creation.

Chapter 6: Must-Visit Landmarks and Attractions

Basilique Notre-Dame de la Garde

Dear fellow traveler, let us ascend to the majestic heights of the Basilique Notre-Dame de la Garde—a sanctuary that crowns the city of Marseille with grace and watchful protection. As we make our way up the hill, we feel a sense of reverence, for this sacred place has been a beacon of hope and solace for generations of Marseille's residents and sailors.

The basilica stands tall and proud, a testament to the devotion of the people and the strength of their faith. Its Neo-Byzantine architecture, adorned with delicate mosaics and intricate stonework, is a true marvel—a masterpiece that reflects the love and dedication poured into its creation.

As we enter the basilica, the air is filled with a sense of tranquility and reverence. The soft glow of candles casts a warm light on the gilded altars and sacred icons, creating an atmosphere of peace and reflection.

At the heart of the basilica stands the magnificent golden statue of the Virgin Mary, known affectionately as "La Bonne Mère" or "The Good Mother." With outstretched arms, she watches over Marseille and its people, offering her protection and guidance to those who seek her intercession.

The panoramic views from the basilica's terrace are nothing short of breathtaking. The city of Marseille sprawls before us, a tapestry of red rooftops and azure waters stretching out to the horizon. From this vantage point, we gain a new perspective on the city's beauty and the vastness of the Mediterranean that cradles it.

In this sacred space, we find a sense of serenity and connection to something greater than ourselves. Whether we come seeking solace in times of sorrow or gratitude in times of joy, the Basilique Notre-Dame de la Garde opens its arms to all who come with an open heart.

Outside the basilica, we encounter a small chapel dedicated to sailors—the Chapelle des Marins—a testament to Marseille's deep-rooted maritime heritage. Sailors and their families have sought the blessings of the Virgin Mary here, seeking protection and safe voyages across the tempestuous seas.

Château d'If and Frioul Archipelago

Dear fellow traveler, let us set sail to the enchanting Château d'If and the captivating Frioul Archipelago—a maritime adventure that will transport us to a world of historical intrigue and natural wonders amidst the sparkling Mediterranean waters.

As we approach the rugged shores of the Frioul Archipelago, we are greeted by a collection of small islands, each boasting its own unique charm and allure. The azure sea glistens under the golden rays of the sun, inviting us to explore the hidden treasures that lie ahead.

Our first destination is Château d'If—a fortress perched on a rocky island, its history intertwining with tales of legendary characters like Alexandre Dumas' Count of Monte Cristo. As we step foot on this hallowed ground, we are transported back in time, imagining the stories of prisoners and daring escapes that have made this place a symbol of mystery and adventure.

The fortress walls hold secrets and echoes of the past. We wander through the dark corridors and explore the prison cells, each one a silent witness to the resilience and spirit of those who once lived within them. From the top of the tower, we are rewarded with panoramic views of the sea, the Frioul Archipelago, and the city of Marseille in the distance—a breathtaking sight that reminds us of the vastness of the world.

Leaving the captivating history of Château d'If behind, we set our course to explore the beauty of the Frioul Archipelago. Crystal-clear waters beckon us to dive in and discover the underwater world beneath the waves—a paradise for snorkelers and divers eager to explore the vibrant marine life that thrives in these pristine waters.

We hop from one island to another, each one offering a unique landscape and atmosphere. Ratonneau and Pomègues beckon us with their tranquil beaches and peaceful coves, inviting us to bask in the serenity of the Mediterranean's embrace.

At lunchtime, we indulge in a feast of local delicacies—freshly caught seafood, savory bouillabaisse, and sun-ripened fruits—that fill our senses with the flavors of the Mediterranean. The aroma of the sea mingles with the laughter and joy of fellow travelers, creating a sense of camaraderie and shared appreciation for this natural paradise.

As the day draws to a close, we bid farewell to the Frioul Archipelago, taking with us the memories of its beauty and the spirit of adventure that fills its air. The sea breeze carries our thoughts back to the city of Marseille, where the adventures of the day will forever be etched in our hearts.

Marseille Cathedral (Cathédrale de la Major)

Dear fellow traveler, let us venture into the sacred sanctuary of Marseille Cathedral—the resplendent Cathédrale de la Major—a place where faith and art unite in a harmonious symphony of beauty and devotion.

As we approach the cathedral, its imposing presence commands our attention. The Romanesque-Byzantine architecture stands tall, adorned with intricate details and elegant arches that speak of centuries of craftsmanship and reverence.

Stepping inside, we are embraced by an atmosphere of awe and serenity. The sunlight filters through stained-glass windows, casting a kaleidoscope of colors on the stone floors and creating an ethereal ambiance that fills the space with a sense of divinity.

The cathedral's grandeur is matched only by its vastness, with towering columns reaching towards the heavens and a majestic dome soaring high above, seeming to bridge the earthly realm with the celestial skies.

As we walk along the nave, we are captivated by the exquisite mosaics that grace the walls, narrating biblical stories and scenes from Marseille's rich history. Each mosaic is a labor of love, a testament to the artists' devotion and skill in depicting the sacred tales that have shaped the cathedral's significance.

In the choir, we find the resplendent altar, a focal point of devotion and worship. Here, the faithful gather to offer prayers and find solace in the presence of the divine. The intricate carvings and sculptures adorning the altar tell the stories of saints and martyrs, reminding us of the enduring legacy of faith.

Marseille Cathedral also boasts a magnificent organ, whose harmonious melodies fill the space during special ceremonies and religious celebrations. The music resonates in our souls, elevating our spirits and connecting us with the timeless tradition of praise and worship that has echoed through the cathedral's walls for centuries.

Outside the cathedral, a vast esplanade invites us to pause and admire the stunning views of the

Old Port and the sea beyond. The beauty of Marseille unfolds before us, and in this moment, we feel a profound sense of gratitude and wonder for the journey that has brought us to this sacred place.

Palais Longchamp

Dear fellow traveler, let us wander through the grandeur and elegance of Palais Longchamp—a true architectural marvel that stands as a testament to Marseille's appreciation for art, nature, and the enduring legacy of its past.

As we approach Palais Longchamp, we are greeted by an impressive sight—the majestic structure, crowned with a resplendent fountain and flanked by lush greenery, invites us to step into a world of beauty and refinement.

The Palais was built in the 19th century to celebrate the arrival of Marseille's new water supply from the River Durance. It is a harmonious blend of neoclassical and

Renaissance architectural styles, exuding a sense of grace and sophistication.

Upon entering the palais, we find ourselves in a splendid hall filled with natural light and adorned with grand staircases and sculptures that pay homage to the abundance of water. The central courtyard beckons us to explore further, where we encounter the pièce de résistance—the grand fountain.

The Fontaine de Longchamp, a masterpiece of sculpture and engineering, stands at the heart of the Palais. Water cascades from the top, flowing gracefully into ornate basins adorned with mythological figures and allegorical representations of abundance and fertility. The soothing sound of flowing water fills the air, creating a tranquil and meditative atmosphere.

Beyond the palais lies Parc Longchamp, a lush oasis of greenery and tranquility. The park's gardens and pathways invite us to take a leisurely stroll and immerse ourselves in the beauty of nature. Towering trees provide shade, while vibrant flowers add a splash of color to the landscape.

At the end of the park stands the Musée des Beaux-Arts, a treasure trove of artistic masterpieces that span centuries and cultures. The museum's collection features works by renowned artists, inviting us to immerse ourselves in the world of art and creativity.

As we sit by the fountain, surrounded by the elegance of Palais Longchamp and the serenity of Parc Longchamp, we feel a sense of wonder and appreciation for the city's dedication to preserving its heritage and celebrating the beauty of nature.

Fort Saint-Jean

Dear fellow traveler, let us embark on a journey back in time to Fort Saint-Jean—a historic fortress that guards the entrance to the Old Port of Marseille, standing as a sentinel of the city's rich maritime heritage.

As we approach Fort Saint-Jean, we are greeted by its imposing walls and bastions, a reminder of its strategic importance throughout the centuries. The fort's history dates back to the 12th century, and its story is intertwined with the ebb and flow of Marseille's past.

Stepping inside the fortress, we are transported to another era. The ancient stone walls echo with tales of battles and conquests and the footsteps of generations who have walked these hallowed grounds. We feel a sense of reverence for the history that surrounds us, a history that has shaped the destiny of Marseille and its people.

As we explore the fort, we encounter remnants of its military past—cannons, watchtowers, and defensive structures—that offer a glimpse into the strategies used to protect the city from potential invaders. From the top of the fortifications, we are rewarded with sweeping views of the Old Port and the Mediterranean beyond, a reminder of the strategic advantage that Fort Saint-Jean once held.

Beyond its military significance, Fort Saint-Jean also houses cultural institutions, including the Museum of European and Mediterranean Civilizations (MuCEM). The museum, connected to the fort by a modern footbridge, is a celebration of the region's cultural diversity and the interconnectedness of Mediterranean civilizations.

As we walk through the museum's exhibits, we are immersed in a world of art, history, and anthropology, showcasing the rich tapestry of cultures that have flourished along the Mediterranean shores. The blend of ancient artifacts and contemporary art creates a sense of continuity—a reminder that the past and present are forever intertwined.

Outside the museum, we find ourselves in the heart of the fort's interior courtyard—an inviting space where visitors gather to relax and soak in the ambiance of this historic landmark. The sound of trickling water from the fountain adds to the tranquil atmosphere, inviting us to pause and reflect on the passage of time and the enduring spirit of Marseille.

Chapter 7: Museums and Cultural Sites

MuCEM (Museum of European and Mediterranean Civilizations)

Dear fellow traveler, let us step into the cultural tapestry of MuCEM—the captivating Museum of European and Mediterranean Civilizations—a place where the vibrant history and diverse cultures of the Mediterranean come together in a harmonious celebration of human heritage.

As we approach MuCEM, its striking modern architecture stands in beautiful contrast against the historic backdrop of Fort Saint-Jean, creating a visual marvel that speaks to the seamless blending of the past and the present.

Stepping inside, we find ourselves immersed in a world of art, artifacts, and interactive exhibits that tell the stories of the diverse civilizations that have thrived along the Mediterranean shores for millennia.

The museum's galleries unfold like chapters in a grand narrative, each one dedicated to exploring a different aspect of the Mediterranean's rich cultural mosaic. Ancient artifacts and archaeological treasures evoke the glory of civilizations past, while contemporary artworks and multimedia installations shed light on the vibrant expressions of the present.

As we wander through the exhibits, we are captivated by the beauty and complexity of human history. We encounter the wisdom of ancient philosophers, the craftsmanship of skilled artisans, and the resilience of communities that have weathered the tides of time.

The Mediterranean Sea, which has served as a cradle of civilization, becomes a unifying thread that weaves its way through the museum's narrative. We gain a deeper appreciation for the region's interconnectedness—the cultural exchanges, trade routes, and shared histories that have shaped the diverse identities of the Mediterranean's peoples.

Beyond the museum's walls, a breathtaking panoramic view of the sea opens up before us. The sparkling waters of the Mediterranean beckon, inviting us to ponder the vastness of this ancient sea and the stories it holds within its depths.

MuCEM also celebrates the living traditions and contemporary cultures of the Mediterranean through performances, film screenings, and cultural events. In the museum's open spaces, we may encounter artists, musicians, and storytellers who breathe life into the vibrant heritage of the region.

As we bid farewell to MuCEM, we carry with us a newfound appreciation for the interconnectedness of our world—a reminder that, despite our differences, we are united by a shared human heritage that spans generations and continents.

Musée d'Histoire de Marseille (History Museum)

Dear fellow traveler, let us step into the fascinating world of the Musée d'Histoire de Marseille—the History Museum of Marseille—a treasure trove that unveils the ancient tales and rich heritage of this storied city.

As we enter the museum, we are transported back in time to Marseille's earliest days—a journey that spans over 2,600 years of history. The exhibits come alive with artifacts, models, and multimedia displays that narrate the captivating stories of Marseille's past.

The museum takes us on a chronological voyage, tracing the city's evolution from its humble beginnings as a Greek colony to its current status as a vibrant metropolis. We marvel at the ancient relics that have been unearthed from archaeological sites, offering glimpses into the lives of the people who walked these streets centuries ago.

The vibrant history of Marseille unfolds before our eyes—the bustling port, the intermingling of cultures, and the challenges faced by the city in times of war and peace. Each chapter in Marseille's story is a testament to the resilience and spirit of its people.

As we explore the various periods and themes, we encounter the legacies of significant figures who have shaped Marseille's destiny—the visionary leaders, the artists and thinkers, and the everyday citizens whose lives are interwoven into the fabric of the city's history.

The museum's galleries are a reflection of Marseille's diversity, highlighting the contributions of various communities that have called this city home over the centuries. From the ancient Greeks and Romans to the Arab and Jewish communities, Marseille's cultural tapestry is as rich and vibrant as the Mediterranean sea it overlooks.

Outside the museum, we find ourselves in the heart of the city, surrounded by the very streets and landmarks that have played a part in Marseille's story. We feel a sense of kinship with the past, knowing that we are walking in the footsteps of those who came before us.

As we leave the Musée d'Histoire de Marseille, we carry with us a deeper appreciation for the city's heritage and a profound connection to its people. We are reminded that the past is not a distant memory but a living legacy that continues to shape the present.

Musée des Beaux-Arts (Fine Arts Museum)

Dear fellow traveler, let us embark on an artistic journey through the Musée des Beaux-Arts—the Fine Arts Museum of Marseille—a haven of creativity and inspiration that unveils the beauty of human expression across the ages.

As we step inside the museum, we are greeted by a world of artistic masterpieces—a tapestry of paintings, sculptures, and decorative arts that reflect the rich diversity of artistic styles and movements.

The galleries come alive with color, light, and emotion as we encounter the works of renowned artists from different periods and cultures. From the Renaissance masters to the Impressionists, the museum's collection showcases the evolution of artistic expression through the ages.

Each painting is a window into the soul of the artist—a glimpse of their thoughts, dreams, and visions. The brushstrokes convey a myriad of emotions, from the gentle strokes of serenity to the bold flourishes of passion.

Sculptures stand proudly, capturing the beauty of the human form and immortalizing moments of triumph and grace. The delicate details and exquisite craftsmanship leave us in awe of the artist's skill and dedication.

As we move through the museum's halls, we find ourselves drawn to particular pieces that resonate with our own experiences and sensibilities. Art has a way of speaking to each of us in a unique language—a language of the heart and the soul.

Beyond the paintings and sculptures, the decorative arts beckon us with their elegance and craftsmanship. Intricately designed furniture, delicate porcelain, and dazzling jewelry tell stories of opulence and refinement.

The museum's atmosphere is one of contemplation and reflection. Each artwork invites us to pause and ponder—to connect with the artist's vision and to find meaning in the beauty that surrounds us.

Outside the museum, we are surrounded by the vibrant city of Marseille—a city that has long been a source of inspiration for artists throughout history. The colors, the light, and the lively spirit of the city are all captured in the works that adorn the museum's walls.

As we bid farewell to the Musée des Beaux-Arts, we carry with us a deeper appreciation for the power of art to move, to inspire, and to connect us across time and space. We are reminded that the language of art is universal—a language that transcends boundaries and speaks directly to the soul.

Regards de Provence Museum

Dear fellow traveler, let us venture into the captivating world of the Regards de Provence Museum—a hidden gem nestled in the heart of Marseille, where art and history intertwine to celebrate the beauty and spirit of the Provence region.

As we approach the museum, its historic façade and unique location by the Old Port draw us in with a sense of curiosity and anticipation. Once a maritime station, the Regards de Provence has been lovingly transformed into a cultural sanctuary—a place that honors the artistic heritage of Provence and its profound connection to the Mediterranean.

Upon stepping inside, we find ourselves immersed in a world of colors, scents, and textures that evoke the essence of Provence. The museum's exhibits pay homage to the region's artistic legacy, showcasing a diverse collection of contemporary and historical artworks that have been inspired by the landscapes, traditions, and people of Provence.

Paintings by renowned Provençal artists transport us to sunlit lavender fields, olive groves, and charming villages. The brushstrokes capture the play of light on the countryside, inviting us to bask in the timeless beauty of the Provençal landscape.

Sculptures and photographs offer glimpses into the rich tapestry of Provençal life—the bustling markets, the vibrant festivals, and the moments of quiet contemplation that define the rhythm of life in this enchanting region.

One of the highlights of the museum is its open-air terrace, which offers panoramic views of the Old Port and the sea beyond. Here, we find ourselves surrounded by the same landscapes that have inspired generations of artists, creating a profound connection between the art inside the museum and the natural beauty that surrounds it.

As we stroll through the galleries, we encounter not only the works of artists but also the stories of the people who have called Provence home. The museum weaves together art and history, providing a glimpse into the rich cultural heritage that has shaped the identity of this timeless land.

Outside the museum, we are immersed in the vibrant atmosphere of Marseille—the blend of Provençal traditions and contemporary life that permeates the city's streets and neighborhoods.

La Vieille Charité

Dear fellow traveler, let us venture into the heart of Marseille's historic quarter to discover La Vieille Charité—a place that holds the stories of compassion, resilience, and cultural richness that have shaped the city's soul.

As we approach La Vieille Charité, its distinctive architecture and tranquil courtyard capture our attention. This 17th-century complex, designed by the architect Pierre Puget, was once a charitable institution—a refuge for the poor, the homeless, and the vulnerable. Today, it stands as a testament to the enduring spirit of humanity's capacity for kindness and care.

Stepping inside the courtyard, we find ourselves surrounded by the stunning arcades and elegant façades that encircle this beautiful square. The sun bathes the space in a warm glow, inviting us to pause and appreciate the serenity of the moment.

The museum that now occupies La Vieille Charité houses a rich collection of art and artifacts that span different eras and cultures. The exhibits are a celebration of Mediterranean and African art, taking us on a journey through time and space to explore the diverse expressions of human creativity.

Ancient artifacts and archaeological treasures from civilizations long past transport us back to a time of myth and legend. Sculptures and paintings from different cultures invite us to appreciate the beauty and symbolism that have woven the threads of human existence for centuries.

Beyond the artistic riches, the history of La Vieille Charité itself is a compelling tale of transformation. From its origins as a charitable institution to its present-day role as a cultural center, the complex reflects the evolution of Marseille—a city that has embraced its heritage while embracing the world.

The rooftop terrace of La Vieille Charité offers breathtaking views of the surrounding neighborhood—the bustling streets and rooftops of the historic Panier district. From this vantage point, we gain a deeper appreciation for the layers of history and the sense of continuity that binds the past and the present.

As we leave La Vieille Charité, we carry with us a sense of gratitude for the compassion and care that have shaped this place throughout the ages. We are reminded that at the heart of any community lies the enduring spirit of humanity—a spirit that reaches out to uplift and support those in need.

Chapter 8: Outdoor Activities and Nature

Calanques National Park: Hiking and Scenic Beauty

Welcome, dear adventurer, to the breathtaking Calanques National Park—a true paradise where rugged limestone cliffs meet the azure waters of the Mediterranean, creating a landscape of unparalleled beauty and wonder.

Nestled just a stone's throw away from Marseille, this natural gem stretches along the coastline, encompassing a vast expanse of pristine wilderness. Here, nature reigns supreme, offering a sanctuary for hikers, nature enthusiasts, and those seeking solace in the embrace of untouched landscapes.

As we set foot on the well-marked trails, we are captivated by the sheer grandeur of the calanques—deep, narrow inlets carved by the relentless forces of wind and water over millennia. The cliffs rise majestically from the sea, forming a dramatic backdrop against the cerulean sky.

The hiking trails meander through fragrant pine forests, where the air is perfumed with the scent of resin and the chirping of birds adds a symphony to our journey. We are immersed in the natural world, far away from the hustle and bustle of city life, surrounded only by the gentle rustling of leaves and the occasional call of wild creatures.

As we ascend the rocky paths, our efforts are rewarded with breathtaking vistas that leave us in awe. From high vantage points, we gaze upon the sparkling sea below, its waves crashing against the rocky shores in a rhythmic dance of eternal harmony.

The calanques themselves beckon us with their crystalline waters—a haven for swimmers, snorkelers, and kayakers eager to explore the hidden coves and marine life beneath the surface.

With every step, the landscape transforms before our eyes, revealing new wonders and hidden treasures. Along the way, we encounter wildflowers blooming in vibrant hues, delicate butterflies fluttering among the foliage, and elusive wildlife that calls this rugged terrain home.

In the warmer months, the sun-kissed cliffs become a haven for sunbathers, while cooler temperatures in the shoulder seasons make hiking a joy. Regardless of the time of year, the Calanques National Park remains an ever-changing canvas of natural beauty, drawing us in with its charm and allure.

As the day draws to a close, we find ourselves perched atop a rocky ledge, gazing upon the spectacular sunset—a moment of tranquility and reflection that imprints itself in our memories forever.

Frioul Archipelago: Beaches and Nature Retreat

Dear fellow traveler, let us set sail to the enchanting Frioul Archipelago—a hidden paradise of pristine beaches and untouched nature that awaits just a short boat ride from the bustling city of Marseille.

As we approach the archipelago, a sense of tranquility washes over us—the azure waters and gentle sea breeze invite us to embrace the serenity of this secluded retreat.

The Frioul Archipelago comprises four main islands—Ratonneau, Pomègues, If, and Tiboulen—each with its own unique charm and character.

We begin our exploration on Ratonneau, the largest of the islands, where sandy shores and crystal-clear waters beckon us for a day of beachside bliss. The Plage du Grand Sable, with its fine golden sands, offers a haven for sunbathers and beachcombers, while the Plage du Petit Sable lures snorkelers with its underwater wonders.

For those seeking adventure, hiking trails crisscross the island, leading us through fragrant pine groves and rocky outcrops with panoramic views of the Mediterranean.

Our journey then takes us to Pomègues, a quieter island that feels like a true escape from the world. Here, we wander along rugged coastlines, discovering secluded coves where the sea gently caresses the shore. The untouched beauty of

Pomègues leaves us feeling as if we have stepped into a postcard-perfect paradise.

Next, we visit the iconic Château d'If—a fortress with a storied past that stands proudly on its own island. Made famous by Alexandre Dumas' novel "The Count of Monte Cristo," the Château d'If offers a glimpse into history and an opportunity to immerse ourselves in tales of adventure and intrigue.

As we explore the archipelago, we encounter a diverse array of wildlife, from seabirds soaring above to colorful fish dancing beneath the waves. The Frioul Archipelago is a protected marine reserve, ensuring that its natural beauty and delicate ecosystems remain preserved for generations to come.

The islands are also home to a variety of Mediterranean flora, which paints the landscape with vibrant colors and fills the air with the sweet scents of wildflowers and aromatic herbs.

As the sun begins to set, we find a peaceful spot to watch the sky change hues, casting a warm glow over the archipelago. The stillness of the evening and the soft sound of lapping waves create a moment of serenity, a reminder of the natural rhythms that govern this untouched haven.

Parc Borély: Gardens and Recreational Park

Dear fellow traveler, let us step into the lush embrace of Parc Borély—a haven of tranquility and natural beauty that invites us to indulge in the simple joys of life.

As we enter the park, we are greeted by a symphony of colors and scents—the manicured gardens burst with a kaleidoscope of flowers, while towering trees offer their shade as a respite from the sun's warm embrace.

Parc Borély is a treasure trove of serenity and recreational opportunities where locals and visitors alike come to unwind and bask in the splendor of nature.

We begin our journey with a leisurely stroll along the tree-lined pathways—the gentle rustling of leaves overhead and the soft crunch of gravel beneath our feet create a soothing rhythm that accompanies our every step.

The park's botanical gardens are a delight for the senses—roses in full bloom release their sweet perfume into the air, while vibrant beds of seasonal blooms create a living tapestry that changes with the passing seasons.

Nearby, a serene pond mirrors the beauty of the surrounding landscape, inviting us to sit by its edge and reflect on the tranquility that envelops us.

For those seeking a bit of excitement, the park offers a variety of recreational activities. The expansive green lawns are perfect for picnics, frisbee games, or simply lying down and gazing at the passing clouds.

As we move deeper into the park, we encounter a picturesque lake where pedal boats glide gracefully on the water's surface. The laughter of children and the playful splashes of water add to the joyful ambiance of this recreational oasis.

Beyond the gardens and the lake, we find the Parc Borély Velodrome, a place where cycling enthusiasts gather to ride along well-maintained tracks and embrace the freedom of the open air.

Watersports and Boat Tours

Dear fellow traveler, let us dive into the exhilarating world of watersports and boat tours—a thrilling adventure that unveils the wonders of the Mediterranean Sea and the coastal beauty of Marseille.

For water enthusiasts and adventure seekers, Marseille offers a playground of exciting activities that cater to every taste and skill level.

Let us begin with the adrenaline-pumping watersports that will get our hearts racing. Windsurfing and kiteboarding are popular choices for those who seek the thrill of riding the waves and harnessing the power of the wind. The sweeping bay of Marseille provides the perfect conditions for these high-energy water activities, and the skilled instructors are ready to guide us on our exciting journey.

For a more leisurely yet equally captivating experience, we can try stand-up paddleboarding—an opportunity to glide serenely over the clear waters, enjoying a unique perspective of the coastline and the city. As we paddle along, we might even spot some of the marine life that calls the Mediterranean home, adding a touch of wonder to our aquatic adventure.

Diving enthusiasts will find themselves in paradise, as the waters around Marseille are teeming with underwater marvels. Scuba diving excursions take us to vibrant reefs and fascinating shipwrecks, where we can encounter colorful fish, graceful rays, and even the majestic seahorses that inhabit the sea bed.

But the adventure does not end on the water's surface. Marseille's boat tours offer an entirely different perspective of the city and its breathtaking calanques. From a boat, we can marvel at the rugged cliffs, hidden coves, and pristine beaches that line the coastline.

The Calanques boat tour, in particular, is a must-do experience. Drifting through the turquoise waters, we are enveloped by the majestic beauty of the limestone cliffs rising dramatically from the sea. The boat's captain regales us with tales of local history and geology, giving us a deeper appreciation for the natural wonders that surround us.

As the sun sets, we can choose to embark on a magical sunset boat tour. The glowing hues of the sky paint a mesmerizing canvas, creating a romantic and unforgettable moment to cherish.

Chapter 9: Food and Dining in Marseille

Introduction to Provençal Cuisine

Dear fellow traveler, let us embark on a culinary journey through the enticing world of Provençal cuisine—a gastronomic delight that captures the essence of the Provence region in the south of France.

Provençal cuisine is a celebration of the Mediterranean's bounty, where fresh, seasonal ingredients take center stage and traditional recipes are lovingly passed down through generations.

As we sit down to a Provençal meal, we are greeted with an array of colors and aromas that awaken our senses. The dishes are a reflection of the region's sunny climate, fertile lands, and vibrant cultural tapestry that has shaped its culinary identity.

At the heart of Provençal cuisine is a reverence for simplicity and purity. Fresh vegetables, herbs, and olive oil are the stars of many dishes, creating a symphony of flavors that dance on the palate.

The region's fertile lands give rise to an abundance of vegetables, such as tomatoes, eggplants, zucchinis, and peppers—ingredients that form the foundation of classic Provençal dishes like ratatouille, a delightful medley of roasted vegetables bursting with Mediterranean goodness.

Seafood plays a significant role in the cuisine as well, reflecting the coastal location of the Provence region. Fresh fish, such as sea bream, sea bass, and red mullet, are grilled to perfection, allowing their natural flavors to shine through.

And let us not forget the rich and earthy flavors of Provençal stews and soups, such as bouillabaisse—a hearty fisherman's stew that warms the soul and beckons us to savor every spoonful.

As we explore the Provençal table, we encounter the bright and bold flavors of aromatic herbs like thyme, rosemary, and oregano, which infuse dishes with their fragrant essence.

Olives, an essential element of Provençal cuisine, find their way into various dishes, whether as a garnish or in the form of rich, golden olive oil that elevates every morsel it touches.

To accompany these delectable dishes, Provençal wines, such as Côtes de Provence and Bandol, offer a delightful complement. Sipping on a glass of local rosé wine as we savor the flavors of the region is a truly blissful experience.

And no Provençal meal is complete without indulging in the exquisite sweets that grace the dessert table. Delicacies like tarte tropézienne, a heavenly pastry filled with cream, and calisson, an almond and candied fruit confection, satisfy our sweet cravings with their heavenly flavors.

Must-Try Marseille Specialties

Dear fellow traveler, let us savor the delectable delights that Marseille's culinary scene has to offer—a treasure trove of specialties that reflect the rich flavors and cultural diversity of this vibrant city.

1. **Bouillabaisse**: A Marseille classic, bouillabaisse is a sumptuous fisherman's

stew that captures the essence of the Mediterranean Sea. Made with an assortment of fresh fish and shellfish and flavored with saffron and garlic, this hearty dish is a true taste of coastal indulgence.

2. **Fougasse**: A beloved Provençal bread, fougasse is a delightful treat that comes in various shapes and flavors. From simple herb-infused versions to those filled with olives or cheese, this savory bread is perfect for savoring on its own or pairing with a selection of local cheeses and cold cuts.

3. **Panisse**: Crispy on the outside and tender on the inside, panisse is a chickpea-flour fritter that delights both locals and visitors

alike. Often served as a delicious street food snack, these golden nuggets are an irresistible way to experience the taste of Marseille.

4. **Pieds et Paquets**: For the adventurous foodie, pieds et paquets is a must-try dish. This traditional delicacy consists of sheep's feet and tripe, served with a stuffing of herbs and spices. Though it may sound unconventional, the flavors of this dish are deeply rooted in Marseille's culinary heritage.

5. **Navettes**: No culinary exploration of Marseille is complete without trying the iconic navettes—a boat-shaped biscuit with hints of orange blossom. Traditionally made to celebrate

Candlemas, these sweet treats are now a beloved snack enjoyed year-round.

6. **Aioli**: Aioli is not just a condiment; it is a cherished cultural tradition in Marseille. A garlic and olive oil-based sauce, aioli, is typically served with boiled vegetables, boiled fish, and eggs. It is a true testament to the simplicity and beauty of Provençal flavors.

7. **Pastis**: To complete our culinary journey, we must raise a glass of pastis—a quintessential anise-flavored aperitif that holds a special place in Marseille's heart. Served with water to create a refreshing drink, pastis are the perfect way to toast new friendships and unforgettable memories.

With each bite and sip, we immerse ourselves in the rich tapestry of Marseille's gastronomy—a delightful fusion of flavors and traditions that beckons us to celebrate the art of savoring the simple pleasures of life.

Top Restaurants and Street Food

Dear fellow traveler, let us embark on a gastronomic adventure through Marseille's top restaurants and indulge in the delightful street food that graces the bustling streets of this vibrant city.

Top Restaurants

1. **Le Petit Nice Passedat**: Perched on the waterfront with stunning sea views, this three-Michelin-starred restaurant is a culinary haven created by Chef Gérald Passedat. With a focus on fresh seafood and Mediterranean flavors, every dish is a masterpiece that celebrates the bounty of the sea.

2. **Chez Fonfon**: Nestled in the heart of the Vallon des Auffes, Chez Fonfon is an iconic Marseille restaurant that has been serving classic bouillabaisse for generations. The ambiance is charming and relaxed, offering a perfect setting to savor the flavors of this Marseille specialty.

3. **Le Malthazar**: Located in the vibrant Vieux Port area, Le Malthazar combines a trendy ambiance with a menu inspired by Provençal and Mediterranean cuisine. From fresh seafood to flavorful meat dishes, every bite is a delight that celebrates local ingredients.

4. **L'Épuisette**: With its enchanting seaside terrace and impeccable service,

L'Épuisette offers a dining experience that is both refined and authentic. The menu showcases the best of Provençal and Mediterranean flavors, ensuring a memorable meal by the sea.

5. **La Boîte à Sardine**: A hidden gem tucked away in the Panier district, La Boîte à Sardine is a small, charming restaurant that delights seafood enthusiasts with its creative dishes and warm atmosphere.

Street Food Delights

1. **Panisses**: As we wander through the streets of Marseille, we must indulge in a taste of panisses—a crispy, deep-fried chickpea fritter that is a popular street food snack in the city.

2. **Pissaladière**: A Provençal take on pizza, pissaladière is a savory tart topped with caramelized onions, anchovies, and olives—a flavorful treat that's perfect for a quick bite on the go.

3. **Chichi Frégi**: At the local markets and festivals, we'll find chichi frégi—a delectable fried dough pastry sprinkled with sugar and enjoyed warm. This delightful sweet treat is a favorite among locals and visitors alike.

4. **Socca**: A true taste of Marseille, socca is a chickpea pancake cooked in a wood-fired oven until it becomes crispy on the outside and tender on the inside. This traditional street food snack is a must-try culinary experience.

5. **Navettes**: As we explore the historic streets of Marseille, we'll come across boulangeries offering the iconic navettes. These boat-shaped biscuits are flavored with orange blossom and are the perfect sweet treat to accompany our adventures.

Best Cafés and Bakeries

Dear fellow traveler, let us savor the charm and flavors of Marseille's best cafés and bakeries—a delightful array of places that serve up the perfect combination of delightful treats and warm ambiance.

Best Cafés

1. **Café de l'Abbaye**: Nestled in the picturesque neighborhood of Cours Julien, Café de l'Abbaye exudes bohemian charm and artistic vibes. This cozy café is a haven for coffee lovers and offers a delightful selection of pastries and light bites to accompany our favorite brew.

2. **Café de la Banque**: Located in the heart of the Panier district, Café de la Banque

boasts a rich history and a delightful terrace that offers views of the vibrant streets. Here, we can enjoy a traditional French breakfast of croissants and coffee, immersing ourselves in the lively atmosphere of this iconic café.

3. **Café de la Plage**: As the name suggests, this charming café is just steps away from the beach, making it the perfect spot to enjoy a leisurely coffee or a refreshing drink while gazing at the Mediterranean Sea. The relaxed ambiance and friendly service make it a favorite among locals and visitors alike.

4. **Mama Shelter**: A stylish rooftop café with panoramic views of the city, Mama Shelter is an ideal spot to relax and

unwind. With a trendy ambiance and a menu that offers a blend of Mediterranean and international flavors, we can enjoy a delightful meal accompanied by the best views of Marseille.

5. **La Samaritaine**: Established in 1847, La Samaritaine is a historic café that exudes old-world charm. Here, we can savor the rich aroma of freshly brewed coffee and indulge in delectable pastries, taking a step back in time while immersing ourselves in the present moment.

Best Bakeries

1. **Maison Saint-Honoré**: This beloved bakery is known for its exceptional range of traditional French pastries and bread. From flaky croissants to mouthwatering éclairs, each treat is a masterpiece that showcases the artistry of the bakers.

2. **Boulangerie Pâtisserie du Panier**: In the heart of the Panier district, this charming bakery offers an array of artisanal bread and delightful pastries. It's the perfect place to pick up a baguette or a sweet treat as we explore the historic streets of Marseille.

3. **Au Four des Navettes**: A true Marseille institution, this bakery is renowned for its authentic navettes—the boat-shaped

biscuits flavored with orange blossom. These delightful biscuits are a delightful souvenir to bring back home or enjoy on the go.

4. **Boulangerie Pâtisserie Uzureau**: For those seeking gluten-free options, Boulangerie Pâtisserie Uzureau is a haven of delicious gluten-free bread and pastries. Here, we can enjoy traditional French treats without compromising on taste or quality.

5. **Boulangerie de la Plaine**: Located in the lively Cours Julien area, Boulangerie de la Plaine offers a delightful range of bread, pastries, and cakes. The bakery's cozy interior and friendly staff make it a

wonderful spot to indulge in our favorite treats.

Chapter 10: Shopping in Marseille

Local Markets and Flea Markets

Dear fellow traveler, let us immerse ourselves in the vibrant atmosphere of Marseille's local markets and flea markets—a delightful tapestry of sights, scents, and sounds that showcase the city's rich cultural heritage and lively spirit.

Local Markets

1. **Marché de la Plaine**: Located in the bohemian Cours Julien area, Marché de la Plaine is a bustling market that comes to life every Tuesday, Thursday, and Saturday. Here, we can wander through stalls filled with fresh produce, artisanal cheeses, fragrant herbs, and vibrant

flowers. The market's lively ambiance and diverse offerings make it a favorite among locals and visitors alike.

2. **Marché du Vieux Port**: Set against the backdrop of the iconic Vieux Port, this daily market is a treasure trove of Provençal specialties and Mediterranean delights. From freshly caught fish to colorful fruits and vegetables, the market offers a sensory feast that embodies the essence of Marseille's culinary heritage.

3. **Marché de Noailles**: Nestled in the diverse Noailles neighborhood, this vibrant market is a celebration of multiculturalism. Here, we can explore an array of spices, exotic fruits, and international products from around the

world. The lively atmosphere and the mingling of diverse cultures make it a unique and enriching experience.

4. **Marché des Capucins**: Located in the Belsunce district, Marché des Capucins is a hidden gem that offers a wide range of products, including textiles, household items, and fresh food. The market's authentic ambiance and friendly vendors make it a wonderful spot to immerse ourselves in the local way of life.

Flea Markets

1. **Marché aux Puces de la Belle de Mai**: As we step into this sprawling flea market, we are transported to a treasure trove of vintage finds and unique collectibles. From antique furniture to quirky trinkets, the market offers an eclectic mix of items that reflect Marseille's history and artistic flair.

2. **Brocante du Cours Julien**: Held every Sunday in the artistic Cours Julien neighborhood, this charming flea market is a haven for art lovers and vintage enthusiasts. Here, we can discover unique artworks, vintage clothing, and one-of-a-kind pieces that reflect the creativity and craftsmanship of the city.

3. **Marché aux Livres**: For book lovers, this delightful book market on the Quai des Belges is a must-visit. Here, we can browse through a collection of new and second-hand books, ranging from classic literature to contemporary works, as well as rare editions and niche publications.

4. **Vide-Greniers**: Marseille hosts various vide-greniers (attic sales) throughout the year, where locals set up stalls to sell their pre-loved treasures. These events offer an opportunity to find hidden gems and interact with friendly locals who share stories about their cherished belongings.

Unique Souvenirs to Bring Home

Dear fellow traveler, let us discover the unique souvenirs that Marseille has to offer—a treasure trove of delights that will forever remind us of the enchanting moments we spent in this captivating city.

1. **Savon de Marseille (Marseille Soap)**: One of the city's most iconic souvenirs, Marseille soap is a timeless symbol of tradition and craftsmanship. Made with natural ingredients and scented with delicate fragrances, these beautifully wrapped bars of soap make for a thoughtful and practical keepsake.

2. **Navettes**: A true taste of Marseille, navettes are boat-shaped biscuits flavored

with orange blossom. These delightful treats are not only delicious but also rich in history, making them a meaningful souvenir to bring back home or share with loved ones.

3. **Santons**: These handcrafted figurines depict characters from traditional Provençal nativity scenes. Whether it's the shepherd, the baker, or the fisherman, each santon holds a special charm that captures the essence of Provençal culture.

4. **Provençal Fabrics**: Marseille's markets and boutique shops offer a wide range of vibrant Provençal fabrics, adorned with colorful patterns and motifs. These fabrics can be used to create unique home decor pieces or stylish accessories, making them

a wonderful way to infuse a bit of Marseille's charm into our everyday lives.

5. **Artisanal Pottery**: From delicate ceramics to rustic earthenware, Marseille is home to talented artisans who create stunning pottery pieces. Bowls, vases, and decorative items adorned with intricate patterns and Mediterranean colors make for unforgettable souvenirs to adorn our homes.

6. **Local Wines**: Marseille's proximity to the renowned Provence wine region means that we can bring home bottles of exquisite rosé wines and full-bodied reds that capture the flavors of the Mediterranean terroir.

7. **Provençal Herbs and Spices**: The fragrant herbs and spices found in Marseille's markets are a delight for any food enthusiast. From herbes de Provence to lavender buds, bringing home a selection of these aromatic treasures will allow us to add a touch of Provençal flair to our culinary adventures.

8. **Vintage Postcards and Prints**: To capture the city's timeless beauty, vintage postcards and prints featuring iconic Marseille landmarks and coastal vistas make for charming souvenirs that evoke the nostalgia of days gone by.

High-End Shopping Districts

Dear fellow traveler, let us explore the high-end shopping districts of Marseille—a haven for luxury shopping and indulgence, where the allure of fashion, sophistication, and elegance beckon.

1. **Rue Paradis**: This prestigious street in the city center is a paradise for luxury shopping. Here, we can find renowned fashion houses, upscale boutiques, and exquisite jewelry stores. The elegant ambiance and the exquisite selection of designer labels make Rue Paradis a must-visit for those seeking the finest in fashion.

2. **Rue Grignan**: Located in the chic neighborhood of Le Cours Julien, Rue Grignan is a delightful avenue lined with art galleries, designer shops, and stylish boutiques. From high-end fashion to unique pieces by local designers, this street offers a sophisticated shopping experience with a touch of artistic flair.

3. **Les Terrasses du Port**: This modern shopping center is a waterfront gem that houses a curated selection of luxury brands. The sleek design, panoramic views of the harbor, and variety of upscale stores create a captivating shopping experience.

4. **Galeries Lafayette**: Situated in the historic La Bourse building, Galeries

Lafayette is a renowned department store offering a wide range of luxury brands, fashion, and accessories. The grand architecture and the exceptional selection of high-end products make it a destination for indulgent shopping.

5. **Centre Bourse**: This shopping center in the heart of Marseille boasts an array of upscale boutiques and international luxury brands. From designer fashion to fine jewelry, Centre Bourse provides a shopping haven for those seeking refined tastes.

6. **Le Panier**: Although known for its bohemian vibe and artistic flair, Le Panier also hides charming boutiques and concept stores offering unique high-end

fashion pieces and artisanal creations. Exploring the winding streets of this historic neighborhood may lead to the discovery of hidden gems.

Chapter 11: Nightlife and Entertainment

Bars and Pubs with a View

Dear fellow traveler, let us raise our glasses to the enchanting bars and pubs in Marseille that offer not only delightful libations but also breathtaking views of the city's picturesque landscapes.

1. **Le Ciel**: Perched on top of the luxurious Radisson Blu Hotel, Le Ciel offers a rooftop bar experience like no other. From this vantage point, we can marvel at panoramic views of the Vieux Port, the Basilique Notre-Dame de la Garde, and the glistening Mediterranean Sea. As the sun sets, the sky transforms into a canvas

of vibrant colors, creating a magical ambiance that makes every sip even more memorable.

2. **Bar Henriette**: Located on the rooftop of the InterContinental Marseille-HHotel Dieu, Bar Henriette provides a stunning view of the historic Panier district and the old harbor. The chic and contemporary design of the bar complements the magnificent scenery, making it an idyllic spot to unwind and enjoy a cocktail or a glass of fine wine.

3. **Les Ruches du Vieux-Port**: Tucked away on the rooftop of La Cité Radieuse, designed by the renowned architect Le Corbusier, Les Ruches du Vieux-Port is a rooftop bar with an artistic touch. From

here, we can admire the city's skyline, including the iconic Basilique Notre-Dame de la Garde and the azure sea, while sipping on innovative cocktails inspired by Provençal flavors.

4. **Le Bar de la Marine**: Situated on the historic Vieux Port, Le Bar de la Marine offers a front-row seat to the city's vibrant maritime activity. With the picturesque boats bobbing in the harbor and the reflection of the city lights on the water, this bar exudes a timeless charm that captivates every visitor.

5. **La Caravelle**: Nestled on the Quai du Port, La Caravelle is a classic pub with a terrace that provides splendid views of the bustling Vieux Port. Here, we can enjoy a

refreshing beer or a glass of local wine while soaking in the lively atmosphere of this iconic harbor.

6. **Bar du Mucem**: Located within the striking architecture of the MuCEM, the Bar du Mucem offers an unbeatable view of Fort Saint-Jean and the Mediterranean Sea. The sleek and contemporary design of the bar complements the surrounding landscape, making it an inviting spot to enjoy a drink and admire the beauty of Marseille's waterfront.

Live Music and Concert Venues

Dear fellow traveler, let us tune in to the vibrant music scene of Marseille—a city that beats to the rhythm of diverse melodies and where live music venues come alive with soulful performances and electrifying concerts.

1. **Le Silo**: Housed in a former grain silo, Le Silo is a renowned concert hall that hosts a variety of musical acts, from international artists to local bands. With its excellent acoustics and capacity to hold a large audience, Le Silo promises a memorable concert experience.

2. **Le Moulin**: A beloved institution in Marseille, Le Moulin is a historic concert venue that has witnessed countless

memorable performances over the years. From rock and indie bands to electronic and hip-hop acts, Le Moulin attracts music lovers of all tastes.

3. **Espace Julien**: This versatile venue showcases a diverse range of events, including live music concerts, comedy shows, and cultural performances. With its vibrant atmosphere and eclectic programming, Espace Julien offers an immersive experience for music enthusiasts and entertainment seekers alike.

4. **Dock des Suds**: Known for its eclectic programming and multicultural events, Dock des Suds is a melting pot of musical genres and cultural influences. From

world music to reggae, jazz to electronic beats, this unique venue brings together artists from around the globe for unforgettable performances.

5. **L'Affranchi**: Nestled in the heart of the Belle de Mai neighborhood, L'Affranchi is a small yet vibrant concert venue that champions local talent and emerging artists. Here, we can experience intimate concerts and discover new sounds that reflect the dynamic spirit of Marseille's music scene.

6. **Le Poste à Galène**: With its underground ambiance and dedication to promoting indie and alternative music, Le Poste à Galène is a haven for music enthusiasts seeking unique and edgy performances.

From rock bands to experimental acts, this venue is a place to immerse ourselves in the cutting-edge of the music world.

7. **Café Julien**: This charming café in the Cours Julien area doubles as a live music venue, offering intimate performances by local artists and bands. Café Julien's cozy setting and warm atmosphere create an inviting space to enjoy live music in an intimate setting.

Marseille's Vibrant Nightclubs

Dear fellow traveler, let us dance the night away in Marseille's vibrant nightclubs—a city that comes alive after dark with electrifying beats, pulsating rhythms, and a lively atmosphere that promises an unforgettable nightlife experience.

1. **Le Rowing Club**: Perched on the edge of the Vieux Port, Le Rowing Club offers stunning views of the harbor and the iconic Basilique Notre-Dame de la Garde. This elegant nightclub transforms into a lively dance floor, where DJ sets and live music keep the party going until the early hours of the morning.

2. **Le Cabaret Aléatoire**: Located within the dynamic Friche la Belle de Mai cultural

complex, Le Cabaret Aléatoire is a favorite among the city's underground music enthusiasts. Hosting a diverse range of electronic, techno, and indie music events, this nightclub is a haven for those seeking cutting-edge beats and a vibrant crowd.

3. **Baby Club**: Situated in the heart of the Cours Julien district, Baby Club is a compact yet lively nightclub that attracts a diverse crowd of music lovers. With a mix of hip-hop, electro, and house music, this venue promises a high-energy dance floor and a fun-filled night.

4. **Le Paradox**: Nestled in the bohemian neighborhood of Le Panier, Le Paradox is a cozy and intimate nightclub that plays

an eclectic mix of music, from retro classics to contemporary hits. The inviting ambiance and friendly atmosphere make it a favorite spot for locals and tourists alike.

5. **Le Lounge**: As its name suggests, Le Lounge exudes an upscale and stylish vibe, making it a popular destination for those seeking a sophisticated night out. With its chic decor and a mix of house, electronic, and R&B music, this nightclub offers an indulgent experience in the heart of Marseille.

6. **Le Molotov**: For those who love alternative and indie music, Le Molotov is the place to be. This hip nightclub hosts live concerts, DJ sets, and themed parties, creating an electric atmosphere that

celebrates the city's alternative music scene.

7. **Le R2 Rooftop**: Located on the rooftop of the Les Terrasses du Port shopping center, Le R2 Rooftop offers not only stunning views of the city but also a fantastic nightlife experience. This open-air nightclub hosts renowned DJs and international artists, making it a hotspot for partygoers looking for an unforgettable night under the stars.

Chapter 12: Practical Information

Currency and Payment Methods

Dear fellow traveler, let us navigate the world of currency and payment methods in Marseille, ensuring that we have a seamless and convenient experience during our travels.

1. **Currency**: The official currency of Marseille, as well as the rest of France, is the Euro (€). It is represented by the symbol "€" and is divided into 100 cents. The Euro comes in both coins and banknotes, with coins available in denominations of 1, 2, 5, 10, 20, and 50 cents, as well as 1 and 2 euros. Banknotes

come in denominations of 5, 10, 20, 50, 100, 200, and 500 euros.

2. **Payment Methods**: Marseille, being a modern and tourist-friendly city, accepts various payment methods to cater to the needs of visitors from around the world. Here are the most common payment methods you can use during your stay:

3. **Credit and Debit Cards**: Credit and debit cards, especially those with Visa, Mastercard, and American Express logos, are widely accepted at most establishments in Marseille. From restaurants and hotels to shops and attractions, using your card for payment is convenient and secure.

4. **Contactless Payments**: Many places in Marseille offer contactless payment options, allowing you to tap your credit or debit card on the payment terminal for quick transactions, especially for smaller purchases.

5. **Cash**: While card payments are widely accepted, it's always a good idea to carry some cash, especially for smaller purchases or when visiting local markets or smaller establishments. ATMs are readily available throughout the city for cash withdrawals.

6. **Mobile Payments**: Some places in Marseille may also accept mobile payment methods, such as Apple Pay or Google Pay, which allow you to make

payments using your smartphone or smartwatch.

7. **Traveler's Checks**: Although less common these days, some larger hotels and banks may still accept travelers checks, but it's advisable to have them in euros to avoid currency conversion fees.

As we embark on our adventure in Marseille, let us be mindful of our spending and keep our financial information safe. It's always a good practice to inform our bank of our travel plans to ensure smooth usage of our cards abroad.

Transportation Tips and Passes

Dear fellow traveler, let us embark on a journey through Marseille with ease and efficiency as we explore the city's transportation options and make the most of our time in this captivating destination.

1. **Transportation Tips**: Public Transportation: Marseille boasts an extensive public transportation system, including buses, trams, and metro lines, operated by the Régie des Transports Métropolitains (RTM). Public transportation is a convenient and cost-effective way to get around the city and explore its many attractions.

2. **Buy a Transport Pass**: Consider purchasing a Marseille City Pass or a Public Transport Pass to make your travels more convenient. These passes offer unlimited access to buses, trams, and metros within the designated zones, as well as discounts on museums, attractions, and tours.

3. **Single Tickets**: If you prefer flexibility, you can purchase single tickets directly from ticket machines at metro stations or from bus or tram drivers. Keep in mind that single tickets are valid for a limited duration and for a single journey.

4. **Validate Your Ticket**: Don't forget to validate your transport ticket at the beginning of your journey, either at the

ticket machine or by using the validators inside buses and trams. Failure to validate may result in fines.

5. **Explore on Foot**: While public transportation is excellent, Marseille's compact city center allows for enjoyable exploration on foot. Walking through the winding streets and charming neighborhoods offers a unique perspective on the city.

6. **Ride-Hailing Services**: Ride-hailing apps like Uber are available in Marseille, providing an alternative mode of transportation for those seeking a more personalized journey.

7. **Transportation Passes**: Marseille City Pass: The Marseille City Pass includes unlimited access to public transportation (metro, buses, and trams) within the designated zones, as well as free admission to numerous museums, attractions, and guided tours. It's available in 24-hour, 48-hour, and 72-hour options.

8. **RTM Tickets and Passes**: The RTM offers various ticket options, including single tickets, day passes, and monthly or weekly passes. The Pass Navigo allows unlimited travel on RTM's network for a specific duration.

9. **TER Regional Trains**: If you plan to explore areas outside of Marseille, consider using TER regional trains, which

connect the city with other charming towns and cities in Provence.

Tourist Information Centers

Dear fellow traveler, let us seek the assistance and guidance of Marseille's tourist information centers—a gateway to a wealth of knowledge and resources that will enhance our exploration of this captivating city.

Marseille Tourist Office

The Marseille Tourist Office is a key information center for visitors, providing a wide range of services to make our stay in the city as enjoyable as possible. Located in the heart of Marseille, the main tourist office is a great place to start our journey. Here, friendly and knowledgeable staff can offer valuable advice on attractions, tours, events, and transportation options. They can provide maps, brochures, and city guides to help us navigate Marseille's vibrant streets with ease.

Address: 11 La Canebière, 13001 Marseille, France
 Phone: +33 (0)4 91 13 89 00
Website:https://www.marseille-tourisme.com/en/

Other Tourist Information Centers

In addition to the main tourist office, there are several other information centers scattered throughout the city, including at popular tourist spots, train stations, and airports. These centers offer valuable assistance to travelers and can help with specific queries related to their locations.

Velodrome Stadium Tourist Office

Address: 3 Boulevard Michelet, 13008 Marseille, France

Marseille Provence Airport Tourist Office

Address: Terminal 1, Hall B, 13700 Marignane, France

Gare Saint-Charles Tourist Office (Marseille Central Train Station)

Address: Square Narvik, 13232 Marseille, France

These information centers are equipped to answer questions about accommodations, transportation, events, and activities, as well as provide updates on any special festivals or happenings during our visit.

Chapter 13: Day Trips from Marseille

Aix-en-Provence

Ah, Aix-en-Provence, the charming town that beckons us with its elegant boulevards, historic architecture, and delightful Provençal ambiance. Just a short distance from Marseille, Aix-en-Provence offers a captivating escape into the heart of Provence—a land of artistic inspiration, lush landscapes, and a rich cultural heritage.

Things to See and Do in Aix-en-Provence

1. **Cours Mirabeau**: The lively main boulevard of Aix-en-Provence is a perfect starting point for our exploration. Lined with elegant cafes, fountains, and plane trees, Cours Mirabeau is a delightful place to stroll, people-watch, and savor the authentic Provençal atmosphere.

2. **Vieil Aix (Old Town)**: Lose yourself in the charming streets of Vieil Aix, where historic buildings, art galleries, boutiques, and local markets blend seamlessly with the town's artistic spirit.

3. **Cathédrale Saint-Sauveur d'Aix-en-Provence**: This stunning cathedral is a masterpiece of Gothic and Romanesque architecture. Admire its intricate façade, majestic interior, and beautiful cloisters.

4. **Musée Granet**: Art lovers will find solace in this fine arts museum, which houses an impressive collection of works by renowned artists like Cézanne, Picasso, and Van Gogh.

5. **Atelier de Cézanne**: Step into the former studio of the iconic painter Paul Cézanne, where he worked and found inspiration for some of his most famous works. The studio is now a museum offering insights into the artist's life and creative process.

6. **Les Thermes Sextius**: Treat yourself to a moment of relaxation at Les Thermes Sextius, a spa inspired by the ancient Roman thermal baths. Enjoy the soothing waters, massages, and wellness treatments.

7. **Markets**: Experience the vibrant markets of Aix-en-Provence, such as the daily food market at Place Richelme and the lively flower market at Place de l'Hôtel de Ville. Sample fresh local produce and immerse yourself in the colors and scents of Provence.

Getting to Aix-en-Provence from Marseille

Aix-en-Provence is conveniently accessible from Marseille by various means of transportation:

1. **Train**: Frequent regional trains run between Marseille and Aix-en-Provence, with a journey time of approximately 30 minutes. Trains depart from Gare Saint-Charles in Marseille.

2. **Bus**: Buses also connect Marseille to Aix-en-Provence, offering a comfortable and budget-friendly option for travel between the two cities.

3. **Car**: If you prefer the flexibility of driving, Aix-en-Provence is easily reachable by car from Marseille. The

journey takes about 30–40 minutes, depending on traffic.

Cassis

Ah, Cassis, a coastal gem nestled between breathtaking calanques and the shimmering Mediterranean Sea. This picturesque fishing village is a true haven for nature lovers, offering an enchanting escape from bustling city life.

Things to See and Do in Cassis

1. **Calanques National Park**: Cassis is the gateway to the Calanques National Park, a pristine natural wonderland of limestone cliffs, turquoise waters, and hidden coves. Take a boat tour or go hiking to discover the beauty of these stunning calanques, such as Calanque d'En-Vau and Calanque de Port-Miou.

2. **Cassis Harbor**: Stroll along the charming harbor, filled with colorful fishing boats, vibrant cafes, and lively markets. Enjoy the lively atmosphere and savor fresh seafood delicacies at one of the waterfront restaurants.

3. **Cap Canaille**: Drive or hike up to Cap Canaille, the highest sea cliff in Europe,

for sweeping panoramic views of Cassis and the Mediterranean coastline. The vistas from this vantage point are truly awe-inspiring.

4. **Cassis Beaches**: Relax and bask in the sun on the idyllic beaches of Cassis, such as Plage de la Grande Mer and Plage du Bestouan. These sandy shores provide the perfect spot to unwind and take in the beauty of the azure sea.

5. **Cassis Vineyards**: Explore the local vineyards and taste the renowned Cassis white wine. The region's terroir gives the wine a unique character that pairs perfectly with Provençal cuisine.

6. **Cassis Village**: Wander through the quaint streets of the village, lined with charming boutiques, artisan shops, and art galleries. Don't forget to sample some local specialties like calisson—a delicious almond-based treat.

Getting to Cassis from Marseille

Cassis is easily accessible from Marseille, making it an ideal day trip destination or a charming addition to your Provence itinerary.

1. **Train**: Trains run regularly from Marseille to Cassis, with a journey time of about 25–30 minutes. The train station in Cassis is just a short walk from the village center.

2. **Car**: If you prefer the freedom of driving, the scenic drive from Marseille to Cassis takes approximately 30–40 minutes, depending on traffic.

3. **Boat**: During the summer months, you can even take a boat from the Vieux Port of Marseille to Cassis, enjoying a leisurely

cruise along the coast with stunning views of the calanques.

Avignon

Ah, Avignon, a city steeped in history and culture, with its medieval charm and iconic Palais des Papes (Palace of the Popes). Let us venture to this enchanting city, known for its majestic architecture, picturesque streets, and the famous Pont Saint-Bénézet (Saint-Bénézet Bridge).

Things to See and Do in Avignon

1. **Palais des Papes**: Step back in time as we explore the magnificent Palais des Papes, a UNESCO World Heritage Site and one of the largest Gothic palaces in the world. Wander through its grand halls and courtyards and marvel at the stunning frescoes adorning its walls.

2. **Pont Saint-Bénézet**: Discover the legendary Pont Saint-Bénézet, also known as the Pont d'Avignon, a partially ruined bridge that spans the Rhône River. Enjoy picturesque views of the bridge and the river from the riverbanks.

3. **Avignon's Ramparts**: Walk along the well-preserved city walls and ramparts that encircle Avignon, offering panoramic

views of the city and the surrounding landscape.

4. **Avignon Cathedral**: Visit the Avignon Cathedral, also known as the Cathédrale Notre-Dame des Doms d'Avignon, a beautiful Romanesque-Gothic cathedral with an impressive interior and stunning views from its bell tower.

5. **Place de l'Horloge**: Immerse ourselves in the lively atmosphere of Place de l'Horloge, a central square surrounded by cafes, restaurants, and historic buildings. It's a wonderful spot to people-watch and soak in the Provençal ambiance.

6. **Rocher des Doms**: Take a leisurely stroll to Rocher des Doms, a lovely garden atop

a rocky hill, offering breathtaking views of the city and the Rhône River.

7. **Musée du Petit Palais**: Art enthusiasts will appreciate the Musée du Petit Palais, which showcases an impressive collection of medieval and Renaissance art, including works by Botticelli and Carpaccio.

Getting to Avignon from Marseille

Avignon is easily accessible from Marseille, making it a perfect destination for a day trip or a longer excursion.

1. **Train**: Frequent TGV (high-speed train) services run from Marseille to Avignon, with a journey time of approximately 30

minutes. The Avignon TGV station is just a few kilometers from the city center.

2. **Car**: If you prefer the flexibility of driving, the journey from Marseille to Avignon takes about an hour via the A7 highway.

Arles

Ah, Arles, a captivating town that has charmed the likes of Van Gogh and inspired countless artists throughout the centuries. Let us journey to this ancient Roman city, where history, art, and Provençal culture come together in a harmonious symphony.

Things to See and Do in Arles
1. **Amphitheatre (Les Arènes d'Arles):** Marvel at the impressive Roman

amphitheater, a UNESCO World Heritage Site and one of the best-preserved amphitheaters in the world. Take a walk through history as you explore the grand structure that once hosted gladiator games and other spectacles.

2. **Roman Theatre (Théâtre Antique)**: Delve into the past at the Roman Theatre, another remarkable Roman relic. Admire the well-preserved theater's semicircular seating and stage, which now host modern performances and events.

3. **Place du Forum**: Immerse yourself in the heart of Arles at the Place du Forum, a lively square surrounded by cafes and restaurants. Take a moment to relax and

enjoy the Provençal ambiance while savoring local cuisine.

4. **Saint-Trophime Church**: Visit Saint-Trophime Church, an exquisite example of Romanesque and Gothic architecture. Its intricately carved portal and beautiful cloister are a testament to the town's rich religious heritage.

5. **Vincent van Gogh's Trail**: Follow in the footsteps of the great artist Vincent van Gogh, who found inspiration in Arles. Discover the locations that inspired some of his most famous works, such as "Starry Night Over the Rhône."

6. **Alyscamps**: Wander through the ancient Roman necropolis of Alyscamps, an

evocative and atmospheric site dotted with centuries-old sarcophagi and cypress trees.

7. **Les Rencontres d'Arles**: If visiting in the summer, don't miss the renowned photography festival, Les Rencontres d'Arles. This international event showcases exceptional photography exhibitions throughout the town.

Getting to Arles from Marseille

Arles is easily accessible from Marseille, making it a perfect destination for a day trip or a longer sojourn.

1. **Train**: Regular TER (regional) train services run from Marseille to Arles, with a journey time of approximately 1 hour.

The Arles train station is conveniently located near the town center.

2. **Car**: If you prefer the freedom of driving, the journey from Marseille to Arles takes about an hour via the A54 highway.

Chapter 14: Conclusion

Final Tips and Recommendations

My dear friend, as we prepare to embark on our journey through Marseille and its neighboring treasures, let me offer you some final tips and recommendations to make our experience truly unforgettable:

1. **Embrace the Provençal Spirit**: Allow yourself to be immersed in the rich Provençal culture and way of life. Take time to savor the local cuisine, indulge in the regional wines, and appreciate the beauty of the landscapes that have inspired artists for centuries.

2. **Wander off the Beaten Path**: While exploring the popular attractions is a must, don't hesitate to venture into lesser-known neighborhoods, hidden gardens, and local markets. These off-the-beaten-path experiences often lead to unexpected gems and authentic encounters with the locals.

3. **Capture the Moments**: Marseille is a city of vivid colors, stunning architecture, and breathtaking landscapes. Remember to bring your camera or smartphone to capture the beauty of every moment and create lasting memories of our journey.

4. **Try Speaking French**: Although many locals speak English, making an effort to speak a few basic French phrases can go a

long way in establishing a connection with the people and immersing ourselves in the local culture.

5. **Pack Comfortably**: As we explore the city on foot and navigate through various attractions, be sure to wear comfortable shoes and pack a reusable water bottle to stay hydrated during our adventures.

6. **Respect Local Customs**: As with any travel destination, let's be respectful of the local customs, traditions, and dress code, especially when visiting religious sites or participating in cultural events.

7. **Plan for Leisurely Moments**: While we may have a packed itinerary, let's also plan for leisurely moments to soak in the

ambiance of Marseille. Sip coffee at a sidewalk café, watch the sunset by the sea, or simply sit in a park and observe the daily life around us.

8. **Be Open to Experiences**: Some of the best memories are often created when we are open to trying new things. Whether it's indulging in unique local dishes, engaging in local traditions, or participating in activities we hadn't initially considered, let's embrace every opportunity with an open heart and mind.

Fond Farewell to Marseille

As our time in Marseille draws to a close, my dear friend, let us bid a fond farewell to this enchanting city that has captured our hearts and left us with cherished memories that will linger in our souls.

As we reflect on our journey through the vibrant streets, the historic landmarks, and the hidden corners of Marseille, let us carry with us the warmth of the Provençal sun, the colors of the Mediterranean sea, and the echoes of laughter shared with newfound friends.

Farewell to the bustling Vieux Port, where boats dance on the gentle waves and the scent of fresh seafood fills the air. Farewell to the majestic Basilique Notre-Dame de la Garde, standing tall as a guardian of the city and offering breathtaking views of Marseille's beauty.

Farewell to the charming alleys of Le Panier, where history whispers through every stone, and to the lively Cours Julien, where creativity blooms in the artistry of local talents.

Farewell to the calanques, those hidden marvels of nature where the rugged cliffs meet the azure sea, and to the Provencal markets, where the vibrant colors of fresh produce paint a vivid picture of local life.

As we leave Marseille, let us take with us not just photographs and souvenirs but also the spirit of adventure, the curiosity to explore, and the appreciation for the beauty that lies within every place we visit.

Though we bid adieu to Marseille, the memories we have woven into the fabric of our hearts will stay with us forever. Our journey through this captivating city has enriched us, opened our eyes to new wonders, and ignited a passion for exploration that will continue to guide us on our future adventures.

Thank you, Marseille, for welcoming us with open arms and for sharing your beauty, history, and charm. As we move forward on our journey through life, may the essence of Marseille remain a cherished part of who we are, reminding us of the boundless beauty that awaits us in every place we explore.

Farewell, Marseille, until we meet again. Our hearts are forever intertwined with the magic of your streets, the warmth of your people, and the endless possibilities of discovery you have shown us. Happy travels to all the wonders that lie ahead!

Made in the USA
Las Vegas, NV
05 September 2023